THERE   WILL   BE   ANOTHER   DAY

BY

BANY   M   BEEHARRY

235 Sandhurst Road
Edmonton
London N9 8bd

DEDICATIONS

To my late wife Renuka Jayantee Beeharry

My wife ShradhaKumari Beeharry

Mrs Aheela Mooneeram

My granddaughters Nieshka and Leiana

4

FOREWORD

Out in the open, I came in close touch with nature,
the rivers and the woodland
that surrounded my old village, now almost
swallowed by the thirst for modern and fast living.
Everything became part of me.
I cried with them , I played with them,
I laughed with them.

I missed the birds
and the baby hares when they were not there.
I miss the great Bois de Natte trees,
of beautiful dark purple hue
the wild, spooky and noisy bamboo groves
and those rambling clumps of hibiscus.
I miss the intoxicating fragrance
of the Queens of the Night.

This book therefore puts into poetry my old village,
the well, the rivers and the near-by sea
and those straggly heaps of warm moss-covered
stones,
said to be the untimely graves of runaway slaves,
those clumps of whining bamboos, the spooky place,
that it was before my father dared to settle there.

It was a promise made and a debt, paid.
I feel free now. I feel great.

The sounds of harp and church bells, conch
and running water, have always been with me,
in or out, asleep or awake,
chanting away behind all the wayward noises of
living.
Even now as I write.

THE RISE OF A NEW DAY.

A ray of light in the early morning, wakes me up.
From behind closed windows,
I watch the dark outside,
And the fading stars.

A soft lock of darkness stretches towards the
mountains.
How sweetly, like a woman,
Loose hair, trailing behind her dress,
Over the woodland and the sugar cane fields,
The night floats!

In a slow throbbing ecstasy, life shivers into life.
Leaves strum in the trees, birds chirp
The breeze wakes up to a lithesome frolic
And the bees break into crazy hustling for new
flowers.

Except for that eternal hum, the breath of this
creation,
Hailing the rise of the sun, this serenity has no
word.
There is silence.
There are sounds, only to those who can hear them.

To those who can,
Between the parting night and the rising sun
somewhere

Pass the drowsy valley and clumps of hibiscus in
bloom,
They chant, they enliven and they opiate,

The sounds of conch and the mellifluous flute
The chimes of bells and the breathing of a harp,
The chirping of birds and a long strum in the
leaves,
Perchance an ocean roar and running water,
Or a roll of harmless and gentle thunder.

A ceaseless symphony,
The unsylabled language of the eternal,
The magic that sustains this brittle creation,

6

In them we rise
And in them we ease out into the infinity.
But we always come back.
For we are the threads that bind the eternal to us.

I thrill to celebrate the renewal of this great
will,
A fearless power,
The vanishing vestiges of the nightly scents
And of the queens-of-the-night.

I cling to the joys in the air,
The first flights and songs of the birds and the
blue sky,
Those sunbeams,
Like wandering tinsels filtering through the mist.

A bundle of wonders
That seems to tie the knots on the threads of the
awakening life!
Nothing can be like waking into this aura of mystic
grandeur!
Stay quiet,
Listen to the divine murmurs of the parting night.

JUST   SOME   FLOWERS.

Life can be very hard sometimes.
Love and smiles, colours and flowers
Make us feel better,
And could raise us from the tombs of sinking
feelings.

There are many more things in this world
That bring joys and hope.
Forget the darkness.
As long as there is ignorance, there will be
darkness.
And the rest is always suffering.

Raise your eyes to the blue sky and tell yourself,
I am blessed.
I can still murmur happily in my heart,
A song of enlivening joy that keeps my smile
flowing.

I can still sing a song of love

And see through the guiles of ignorance,
Those sweet fragrances of illusions that bind me
To an uncertain future.

I can still keep the candle of my strength burning
That could make someone somewhere happy.
Fields will grow if I am willing and tears will dry
too.
The sun will shine and flowers will be more
beautiful.

Stop now and then.
Clean the clogs of delusions
And let the river of hope flow.

For life is a beautiful gift.
It is a flower in bloom, the fragrance is there to
be enjoyed.
Do not let it be carried by vain breezes and winds.
It is a sky full of wondrous stars,
Do not let them set in your heart.

It is the way, hold on to it.
It is light and a pointer to ultimate peace.
Do not feed it to the play of illusion.
Not many of us deserve it.
For only the brave sees the sun rise the next day.

8

I SEEK THE TRUTH.

I seek the truth
From where the ideation of this universe
Shivered into a spectacular existence;

Where rivers of wisdom flow unabated
And cascades of ineffable joys drench the air
With unceasing sprays of love and sunshine.

I seek the truth
Where life is not time scaled,
Two-sided or relative,
Where enthralling symphonies are born
That would deluge the air with floods of music.

These I find by diving into my own self,
Following the mystic lamp.
I shake the trees of superstitions
And cull immortal fruits of wisdom.

I churn the frail mind's ocean
And reap rich and multifarious pearls.
I befriend pain and shirk ephemeral pleasures
That like fearsome shadows shroud
The treasure-troves of truth that twinkle at the
bottom.

And all decked, I come
From where the mind dares not to maraud,
And the proud breath sacrifices itself
At the altar of the all encompassing truth.

THE CAGED BIRD.

They say that eternity has no boundary,
No beginning, no end, it is infinite.
But not for me,
I am a bird, a caged bird.

My infinity is only ten inches long and ten inches
wide.
Cloistered, I cry when I am alone,
And back come the echoes to mock me,
Telling me that I am a prisoner.

For no fault of mine,
No crime have I committed,
Unattached for ever.
But I am a prisoner, plucked from my father's home.

Freedom has since become a stranger,
My wings hard, my vision blurred.
But I was once a child of eternity,
Born of light and wisdom
And freedom.

Now and then comes floating like in a blurred dream
The place where I was born:
A beautiful place, sweeping down towards waterfalls
That drenched the air and the blossoms
With flying furls of mist
And sprays of silver dewdrops;

A place of perpetual blooms and light,
Soft music of harps and flutes, bells and conches,
A place where beauty and peace, love and wisdom
First came to be,
And the fleeting vision of my father's face,
Loving in his grandeur, of encompassing beauty.

10

And joy explodes, passed all the dreams of freedom.
What would I do with freedom
Without him?

What would I do with peace
Without him?
And with happiness?
And with love?

In him there are more harvests to be reaped
Than will ever be known in my cage or outside.
My tears taken for singing,
No one knows the pain in my heart.

I yearn to fly close to the blue sky
Where clear clouds dance in the aureate air
And sounds of harmless storms and gentle breezes
blend.

Sometimes in the early dawn,
When peace lies heavy on the eyes of my abductor,
I wake up and watch the first smiles of the day
Seeping through the closed curtains.

I know the sun.
I know the moon and I know the stars.
I was there when my father blew into a handful of
dusts
And the dark space exploded into a crazy riot of
colours,

Frames and forms and tinsels of twinkling lights.

When in the dark, the stars shed no light though,
The moon stays behind veils of still clouds
And the valleys are restless,
I would hear his voice calling,
For he loves me, my father.
I know he cries every time I leave home.

But he cannot fetch me, I am beyond his reach.
I am a prisoner.
For some, I am light, darkness will follow my
departure.
For others, I am peace and happiness
And gloom will sweep the sunlit valleys.

Without me this cage would be empty;
The sun will not rise, the day will not be bright
And the night will never be day, the stars will
cease to be.
The rivers and the brooks will dry.

And this beautiful garden will not be.
They are because I am.
Cry not for me, I am a willing prisoner.
I gave up my freedom for the dream of my father.

WAIT

I waited for the rose buds to bloom
And suddenly the flowers, like butterflies
Rise from the field of ineffable mystery,

An explosion of indestructible beauty
Tender petals,
Weaving garlands of happiness
Love and hope in the heart
And mind.

I waited for the sun to rise
And suddenly
The pale sky lit,
An exuberance of multicoloured light,
A glow that shattered the thunder clouds' vaunts.

I waited for the summer rain
And it poured
And poured,
An endless fall of tenderness from the sky.

And I abandoned myself to the warm
And immense shower of love,
A transcendental bliss.

To wait is not always to waste time.
Things come in their proper time.
To wait is to have faith,
To watch the raising of the curtains on this cosmic
creation.

Neither you
Nor me
Can force the sun to rise
Or to set
Or to force the breeze to blow.
The mist will always move to the hill tops
And saunter around the mountains.

Waiting is to reach out to the infinity.
You realise that life
The chores and the sores,
The blossoms and the thorns are all the same,
Both bred and fed from the same bush.
Some call it thorns, others flowers.

We are the bush,
And the pains and the pleasures our own creations
Children of our actions and reactions.
Accept them and live in peace,
For they will not stop coming,
Not in this world!

Reject them,
And only tears and blood flow
From the flower of ignorance.
Now and then for the sake of peace,

We need to learn from our thorns too.
For sitting in a house of fragrance does not always
Make us smell fragrant.

I CELEBRATE

I celebrate the cosmos with its infinite
Multitude of suns, moons, stars and planets.

I celebrate this lovely and exuberant world
With its blue sky, and oceans,
Its dark thunder clouds, mountains and rivers,
Its flowers, brooks and hills.

I celebrate the known and I celebrate the unknown.
I celebrate he who made them all,
For he who made them, made them into one whole:
An inseparable mosaic.

I salute the greatest of all the marvels:
Man! the home of the infinite, of infinite beauty.
For to him was given the gift
To comprehend the infinite,
To see, to hear, and to love the whole.

To him was given the gift
To seek the eternal home of wisdom,
And having found which, time ceases to scare,
Barred and cooped up in the house of gross matter,
A toothless moron.

I NEED TO KNOW

I have eyes,
But I cannot see what I need to see.
I have ears,
I cannot hear what I need to hear.

What I see and hear
Have got me no further than
From where I was in the first place.
Stunted!

I need to see where the road of my life is leading,
Beyond this perishable piece of flesh and bones.
There the senses,
Pretentious and ignorant, cannot reach.
They die a natural death,
And time ceases to vaunt the sad tears it left
behind.

I need to know
What is that light burning in the distance
Telling me of subtle places,
Where immortality is never too far,
And always is.

I need to know
Who speaks in the silence of the night
Reproaching me.
Wake up, I am here, the one you are looking for.
And you are sleeping?

Nothing seems real here, dying before I reach them.
How can I trust anything?
Or hold to something
That cannot hold itself?

Wisdom lies somewhere,
Beyond the fringe of this handful of mortal dusts.
I need to know the way.
It's all around me, calling.
Calling!

Yet I am willfully deaf
And blind.
Cloistered, I die to rise to the blue sky
Like the grounded peacock.

16

WHERE IS THE DIFFERENCE?

You think we are different
Because we look different?

But who knows what unseen forces had moulded us,
Age after age?
Have made us fruits of different trees?
They have made me sour and you sweet.
They have made you sour and me sweet.

Yet both our lives hang on the precarious swings
Of that fleshly pendulum.
When the sun sets, we both look for comfort
In the arms of the nightly slumber.
When our throats are parched,
We both look for the fountain to quench our thirst.

At the vehemence of the nightly nightmares,
We both sit up in bed, dearly wishing for the day to
break.

And when finally the frail pendulum ceases to swing,
We both are forced to tug our tails in
And ease out into that same immense and blind
nothingness,
Leaving behind the pampered pride and hoarded
wealth.

We are like the waters of the fabled well,
Who knows where from we come,
And where to we go.

AWAKENING.

To wake up to the feast of that singing bird
As the sun, in a aura of bristling rays
Rises from the embrace of the receding night,
Is a rare blessing.

Tucked between closed curtains, I celebrate in
silence,
Leaving my mind and my heart to wander,
Drinking from that chalice of passionate warbling.

An explosion of newly found freedom!
A soul entranced, bathed in divine light,

A soul in ecstasy, rising from the age old
ignorance,
Scattering fragments of thousand fettered lives,
Till now unknown.
New untrammeled visions!

Here consciousness is not a prisoner,
Confined behind the prison bars of seeming reality.
Here freedom is free.

New skies bloom and Nature expands,
A soul is enlightened!
Unrestrained!
Wisdom has at last risen to the height of its own
cosmic reality.

Who says that this creation is merely a handful of
scattered stars,
Hills and mountains,
A mug full of oceans and seas?
Not any more;

18

A flutter
And a dance in the heart,
An explosion of songs,
And a wanton exhilaration.

Who can read that singer's outburst?
What poet, strumming on the lyre of his poetical
inspiration
Can match this extravaganza of melodies?

Oh love, words fail
To paint this explosion of gaiety and sounds,
Lights and colours.
Transcendental!
Ineffable!

Lost in listening,
Inebriated,
I shudder, I freeze.
I surrender, happy
To be drowned in that outpouring
Of love, freedom and bliss.

A TRYST WITH THE PAST.

After several years,
I went back home, where once
I decided to bury my tears and heartbreaks.
Many a sordid thing I wanted to forget.

I wanted to see my old village,
The woodlands, the rivers, the well and the old
girls
All dear and cherished memories of my childhood
days.

Very little had survived the onslaught of time,
The trudge of the modern giants.
Remorse filled my heart.

I tried hard to reconcile myself to this new
phenomena
And wondered whether it was not me instead,
Caught into that sweet slumber of a childhood past,
That I was still living in a past that had long
ceased to be.

Yet I could still catch the clear sky
Studded with endless tinsels of star lights,
The tantalizing fragrance of the queen-of-the-
night,
As one after another
Memories of that remote and magical past gently rose
From the slumber inside me.

Love, they say,
True love never dies.
Time passes, it hides between cracks of life
Taking new forms and names, biding its time to bloom
again.
I waited for them all to bloom.
I waited for the touch of my old childhood days.

Those unwritten phantoms of gliding mist
Those stray moon light,
Those flights of birds and those mellow giggles and
chatters
Of the old girls, as clear and as pure as the blue
sky.

20

For that past was not out there lost in the fog of
time
Not at the mercy of the modern ruthlessness,
It was in me,

With me, it had never left me,
In every breath,
Every throb of my heart.

At night when my sleep is deep,
I could hear their plaints and whispers
Telling me to wake up.

Dreams of my childhood loiterings
The rivers, the slopes full of flowers,
Those massive boulders of rocks
That ancient cemetery decked with clear aureate
sunshine
And flowering hibiscus, those aimless strolls
And the flaming flamboyant, they were still all
there,
Deeply embedded into myself.

This is when the past and the present merge.
Who cares what phantasmagoria the past is
Or the present
Or even the future
They never existed for me.

All I know is that I live
I lived
And I will live.
The secret of life is to be and never to cease to
be.
For death is only a bus stop
Where you get off and wait for a change.

THE KNOWERS OF WISDOM.

We think we know what wisdom is.
Those who know remain silent,
Humble like a fruit-ladened tree, their words few,
Their followers fewer,

Their hearts large,
As large as the oceans,
All there to give
Never to stint, to love ever.

Like shooting stars
They glide across the skies of our lives.
Catch them, whoever can.
For they are the embellishers of our souls,
Their wisdom inexhaustible.

Reapers are few and far between.
Prisoners to the senses,
We live like fated flies in the webs of ignorance,
Reluctant to be reprieved.

Like poppy eaters
We loiter aimlessly in sweet delusion.

22

HE WAS BORN FREE.

He was born free a long time ago
When his mind and body were young.

He loved the village lanes
And the busy market towns.
He loved the river walks, the trees and the wild
lakes,
The secret haunts of the mountains.

There he created dreams and destroyed them in
thousands.
There it was where his dreams grew wings;
Like the frolicsome morning shadows,
He raced the breeze to the foot of the hills.

He flew to the gilt land of moonbeams
And bathed in the mellow lakes of sunshine.
There he rode the fast wind horses to the clouds,
Free from prejudices and dogmas.

Like the birds in the trees, he was free,
Free to sing the songs close to his heart,
To fly and plane dangerously in the wind
And dare the vehemence of enigmatic storms.

Who cares what the books say,
As long as his mind was free to dare and explore
And bring home sweet treasures,
Untarnished by short-minded confinements?

But since, he has lost his freedom,
Gradually circumvented by inveterate bookish weeds.
He was imprisoned by many a belief and superstition.

He would rather live behind prison bars
With his mind free to wonder and wander,
Free to love
To reason and to understand,

Than his body free to rove
And his heart and mind condemned to vegetate
In educated darkness.

THIS FRAIL THREAD OF LIFE.

One day perhaps
I shall again write a song
Woven in the tender threads of love,
Full of faith.

One day from the hill stream,
I shall bring down the water of wisdom,
To cool the thirst of this feckless humanity.

Some say life is an easy slide down the hill's side.
For others, it is a battle ground.
We stand between the ravages of heartless rancours,
And the banes
Of warring bullets and blood shed.
And yet we dream of bringing dust down from the
hostile space.

But life is us
And we are life.
We either live or we do not.
We either see or we do not.
This is sign of humanity being pulled back into the
trough

Of the old ignorance.

We are the battlefield
The weapons, the warriors,
And the enemy too, what a fall!
How frail is life.
We shed life to save life.

The violence and the blood we shed,
The tears and the pain are all our own.
So spill not your own blood.
Spare your heart the unwanted violence of hatred.

For life, like a tree, it grows.
Was not the sunshine made for it,
And the breeze and the immortal gift of love
And those beautiful sunrises and sunsets?

24

A SONG REPRIEVED

Oh song, grieve not,
The noise is everywhere,
This world is in a mood to play.

You are fated to be buried alive in a swath of dust.
Your life may be short
And your message never be heard.
But grieve not.

Even the loneliest flower tucked away
In the harshest desert sand has its importance
In God's eyes.
Nothing goes unnoticed.

This world is a busy market place.
Forgive it.
For from somewhere, sometimes in the future
When reason and silence have their own,
Someone, craving for comfort,
Tears in his eyes
And emptiness in his heart,
Someone will lift you from your bed of dusts.

You will then live again, rising from every word
Every note,
Shivering into life like a tender flower
From the bud at the break of dawn.

Your voice will ring in the wind.
Those hills will again echo to the morning sun's
adoration.
And in their hearts, sing the songs
That you sang to them.

The village will resound.
The world will dance.
Rain will fall.
Green grass will grow.
And dark clouds, in the embrace of wondering
moonbeams
Will turn gold.

You will rise fresh from the ash
And fill the aureate air with joy,
That knows no religion, no hatred, no limit.
All will be joy,

Nothing but joy.
The world will be young again,
And innocent smiles will blaze
Like sunbeams.

Darkness will fly.
You will sing.
I will sing
We shall all sing.
For we will be blessed with a new grace,
The grace of a golden age.

26

THE SEVEN DAY LOVE STORY.

Many a year has drifted by
Since last I saw her.
Age has now caught up with me.

She was queuing for a train ticket.
So was I.
I do not remember how the conversation began..
And do you know what?
We became friends....
Just a trifle little more than that perhaps!

Love is like a butterfly, subtle and elusive.
It hovers,
It tempts and it frisks.
And when it lands, we are willing prisoners.

Something tender slowly crept in.
A throb or two in the heart,
Timid flutters sprouting dear little yearnings.

All of a sudden she seemed to be unbearably far...
Strange
How human beings make dreams of sleepless nights
And flowers of unborn buds!

Six days we had together and on the seventh,
I saw her off at the station.
She said thanks
And cried.

As she got into that train, I knew that with every
clatter
The train made,
She would be swallowed into a whirlpool
Of growing distance, a fog of irretrievable love.

Years later,
The memory of something tender,
The curious seven day love story,
Emerged from the flow of time, an aimless flotsam,
Still fluttering with tender feelings.

Life, they say is an unwritten play, we are blank
sheets.
Time the writer, you can never tell what comes
next.
It could shine,
Or it could shower.

Like children, engaged in playing on the shore
Of tears and laughter.
Unguarded,
We exist from one moment to another.

Some memories recede into forgetfulness.
Others, vanquishing the buffets, rise again
From places unknown, full of flowers and fragrances.
And the pen goes on.

I say
If my love is true,
Distance and storms are but trifle scares.
My words are my flowers;

Of them I make a garland, which I float on the river
of time.
Perchance it will survive the storms,
And outwit the distance.

28

MY DAD IS COMING HOME.

After a long wait,
The sun rises in an spotless blue sky.
A thin screen of the last night mist lingers.
Heart on fire with loving anticipation,
Like a timid bird, I sit up in bed.

Eyes on the door,
Still haloed into the grace of a gentle excitement
I sobbed.
My dad is coming!

But the world sleeps, perchance to dream.
A slumber of sweet nothingness,
Where you create castles,
Cross oceans and at will blow hills and mountains
away.

You dance.
You screech now and then with joy
And wake up to a jolting uncertain reality.

It was all a dream.
The tears were fake, drops from fake pain,
A receding chimera
And the joys, dissembling and beyond reach!

But the reality you wake up to, is real.
The injuries bleed real blood.
The mind rankles with real longings, losses and
hurts.
The tears are warm, the desires incomplete.

I know nothing of the beyond.
There the flowers may last for ever
And endless joys blaze forth glints in emblazoned
eyes.

Did not the wise men sing of eternal life
Where birds lark for endless days in vast blue skies
And riots of colorful flowers stay for ever?
My father is coming home to keep me from dreaming,

He is beyond this frail world, pass this starry
firmament,
Pass this pretentious time, a toothless brute that
knows
No remorse.
I know the woods will explode with endless panoplies
of flowers.
The birds will never cease to warble and to choir.

The breeze, laden with treasures of fragrances
Will lighten every heart.
And from the stars,
What mighty cascades of twinkling lights will come
down!

This empty space will glow.
You will laugh and dance.
I will smile.
This world will smile.

There will be peace,
And love, like honey will drip from the honeycombs
Of all hearts.
There will only be joy.

Why fear then when my father is back home.
Not only for me

But for you, you and you.

30

FLY ME TO THE FANTASYLAND.

I am a poet,
Nature is the field of beauty
And wisdom I wallow in.

When the sun is warm
And the weather is peaceful in my mind
And heart,
I make my way across the village woodland.

And there crazily,
Like bees, drunk on the fragrances of flowers,
I stroll aimlessly.
I loiter from one resting place to another;
Near the river
And under the trees where lithesome shades frolic.

There is a secret in that cool possessiveness of the
woodland,
Something hauntingly serene, that invades your mind,
Holds your heart captive.

There I seek those lines of unwritten poetry,
Those unsung notes of music
And stray warblings from this wondrous mosaics.

For poetry is not merely a concoction of breezy
imagination,
Not always invented by the random mind.
Blind and insensitive mind lacking in depth
Is rarely invited into the ball of this inspiring
mystery.

From the lands of fireflies,
From the darkening of the evening sky
And the stray twinkling of wandering star lights,

From the rolling silver sounds of the temple vesper
bells
They come,
And I cull them, one by one, like picking the stars
From the bareness of the tinsel lit space.
These I bind with ligaments of wandering moonbeams.

The choice is endless, an opiating chase of the
elusive butterfly
Where beauty and music
Fragrance and movements combine to make a thrilling
festival.

This I seek,
The unseen source of the pieces and the mosaic.
The transcendental conflagration that burns,
No flame, no heat,
Beyond the tentative reach of this mind.

THE   CROSS.

I stood before the cross.
I saw my father,
Smiling.

I said to him
It is your will
That I am here,
A fragile thread of mortal coil
Bound to these rowdy senses;

A cross on my forehead
And love and knowledge in my heart.
I fear not the whip.
And I fear not the hammer and the nails,
The crunching march of the soldiers
On the cobbled way.

This body will bleed, since it is your will.
I forgive them
Who bear the whips
And them armed with hammers and nails,
Because they are all yourself,
Different attire, different history.

You are the one who inflicts the pain,
The one who feels the pain,
And the one who sheds tears of comfort.

How strange are your ways!

We are children of infinity, playing on the shores
of time
Picking little flowers and polished stones
By the road side.

Ignorant,
Engaging in petty squabbles and useless warfares.
Sometimes we smile in fake victories,
Sometime we cry in elusive joys,
Blind to your subtle and transcendental play.

Little we know what a great show is going on around
us,
In which you are the director, the producer
The actors and the viewers all in one.

THE VOICE OF MY CONSCIENCE.

The vesper bells have hailed the coming of the
night,
And the village temple is closing.
In the distant darkness above,
Twinkling lights like tears of untainted love
Drop from the eyes of an anxious sky.

I stand still in the shadow of the temple,
And cry.
I always feel like crying when I am late
And the temple is closed.
I hate the rusty screeches of the closing doors.

There is something reproaching in the silence of the
night,
Deep and unsyllabled, coming from inside myself,
The voice of my own conscience.

You are late again,
Now I am beyond your reach.
You have become a mystery to me even,
Unpredictable and unreliable!

You create fear
And who is terrified by it?
You create war and violence
And who gets killed?
You create greed
And who suffers deprivation?

I made my home in your heart,
You move me to a home of wood and stone
Pomp, greed and power, hatred and anger
And at night you shut me in behind cloistered doors.

I created you from myself,
To love you.
Look around, see the world that I made for you.
There is nothing that you can ever think of
That I have not foreseen.

34

And yet at daybreak,
You are the first one to abandon me,
And sell me to the highest bidder,

And leave my back to peel with the laughter of
whips!
I shiver at the thought of how soon you will forget
all about me.

As a mother, I give you love.
As a father, I save you from hunger.
And as a friend, I lighten your days with laughter
and banters.
And yet you turn my home into flats.

But child, remember,
Like to the teacher,
The lessons of life consist of both the ruler and
the book.

This place has a purpose.
You have a purpose.
Life has a purpose.
And when this purpose is forgotten,
The castle of creation crumbles.
The need for its existence becomes untenable.

From the trees to the creeping worm in the warm
moist ground,
The fish in the sea and the birds in the air,
The stars and the moon in the night sky
And the sun in the radiant day,

Every step you take and every breath
Every beat of your heart,
That purpose continues silently to sustain this
creation!

If you think you do not need them,
I can take them back!
Think not the desert is useless
Or those wastelands either.

This place is a mosaic
It is whole only when all the bits are together
And only then this eternal purpose blazes forth
Its transcendence.

The flowers and the fruits appear only when the
tree's purpose
And the life force combine in absolute harmony,
Not before.

The sun comes when the night is ready to leave
And goes when the night and the stars are ready to
return
And nature ready to diffuse the magic of restful
slumbers.

There are no figment in my creation.
These are realities not to be had by force
Or cheat.
Or be reprieved when lost!
Think child, think!

36

THE   WISDOM   OF   THE   DEWDROP.

I stood between a haughty sea
And a drop of dazzling dew, a random pearl of
crystal.

The sea,
Lit by the light of the rising sun,
So wide, but peevish,
So vast, but silently fuming and pretentious!
And yet so beautifully enhanced by a festival of
shooting colour foams.

And a dew drop,
Serene and fearless, facing the uncertainties of its
existence.

The sea will be calm tomorrow.
But tomorrow is far away,
Beyond the portal of thinking, still a wasteland
Or a goldmine.

For the drop of dew, poised on a blade of grass,
There is no tomorrow.
There is only now,

When flowers grow
And the breeze sails boats of coolness,
When hills smile in the sunshine
And beautiful shadows glide like harmless ghosts.

What will be written in the sky tomorrow,
There is no knowing.
Will the birds sing?
Will man survive the battering of this insidious
virus?

But on its string instrument of false calmness and
peevishness,
Storms and destructions

The sea will be there to rhapsodise.

How strange life is.
There is nothing certain here.
We live.
We let live.

We fight one another and shed warm blood of hatred.
How nightmarish it would be if we realize by what we
are being stalked.
Ignorance is a savior sometimes!

Then, then, then....
Only the echoes of our kind and beautiful words will
remain,
Playing in the clear etheric valleys of the love we
leave behind.

For the cuddly dew drop, reality is always two steps
away
At the mercy of the sun
Or the frolicsome breeze.
Only tears and laughter write the lines of its short
and frail life.

Seek not then tomorrow.
It has no form, no sound.
A rowdy chimera, full of fears
And uncertainty, tempered with a breath or two of
smiles.

Carry your life firmly in your hands.
Build your dreams bravely and live them wisely.
For there is no knowing when and where,
You will need to relinquish them.

38

THE PERMANENT AND THE IMPERMANENT

Sometimes lost in the joys of life,
I forget what I came for in this relative world
And what life is about.

I wax in joy for what I see around, the blue sky and
the hills,
Man, the gifted marvel and these unstinting
blessings,
All mine and free.

I willingly make a gift of myself and my will to the
five hungry
And rowdy horses.
I surrender myself to a willful and dissolute
indulge and abuse,

Till the boat of my peace begins to rock, my hope
dodders,
Mocked by my deluded will; joys hurt, the flesh
tired,
The bones ache, the sight, dull and disabled.
The body shrinks, senile and frail.
Gone the beauty that once was , the grit and the
strength.

The indulgence was a false euphoria.
Across thousand acres of mental debris come sharp
flashes
Of warnings from the awakening conscience,
A silent voice, telling me this is not a fool's
paradise.

Locked into a cycle of ceaseless recycling, nothing
is permanent
You, me, everyone, everything is constantly
Easing into the black hole of time.

The earth has always been the winner in claiming the
dusts
That are hers,
No rejoinder, and miraculous reprieves are far
between.
Only to say dusts do not last for ever, only the
spirit is immortal,
The Master Builder Himself, accepting a frame of
living dusts.

For only through the impermanent can the permanent
be known:
This frame is a vehicle, a boat to take the Soul
across the tumultuous
And uncertain torrents of life.
Being is a game of chess between what is permanent
And that which dies.

To achieve immortality, the eternal willingly
accepts a mortal self,

His divine game, His infinite dream.
In search of immortality, even great Saints aspire
for a mortal garb.
The key is knowing how to sift and winnow
The mortal chaff from the immortal.

Like the lotus on the lake, to be in it but not of
it.
That truth I forgot.

40

THE OLD RIVER AND THE OLD ME.

Beyond the ceaseless hush hush of the slumbrous sea
And the strumming of the evening breeze
As it shivered through the village woodland,
Came a call.

Not like the other clamours,
One very dear to my heart,
The gurgling of running water,

A faint rhapsody, that blended the gaiety of my
young days
With its own crystal clear of silver notes,
The voice of an old old friend,
The village river.

The night was far advanced, the village slept.

No hooting pigeon , no whining of the hungry dogs,
Just a serene and breathless tranquility,
A strange air of primal sincerity, innocence
And purity.

After my long absence I dared not budge.
In my heart, I stood by the river in reverent
contemplation,
The same I had played in
And with my friends, splashed naked.

Those were the days of total abandonment,
Lines of inexpressible poetry,
Unwritten songs of straying sunshine and exuberance.

Tear drops flushed my eyes
As I sobbed in silence.
Why cannot everything be eternally young
And thrilling?
Jovial, for ever the same?
I asked myself.

Why cannot beautiful things last for ever?
Why should they like scorpions, carry stings of
inevitable death?
Why cannot we all last for ever,
And ever?
He is wise who can give an answer.

Like the river, I stand bruised by the passage of
time.
What is left of the river, are sinking slabs of
stones,

A sluggish flow of water,
Yellow and stinking, with clogged vegetation.

And me?
A failing frame with blurred eyes,
Coiled backs of the hands, white hair,
A crazy dimwit!

Caught into the flux of a ruthless transmigration
Like the river, I flow too,
Good and bad my banks
And a remote dream of self realization, my final
destination.

There to the sounds of running water,
I had watched the stars in the clear sky,
Sang rapturously to the winds and breeze,
Climbed trees and scared the birds.

Where has the thrill gone,
The strength
And the lithesome run of the clear water?
Where has all the love that I knew, gone?

Now frustrated, sitting on the bank,
I watch a lacerated world go by,
Caught into the spider's web of bitterness,
Hatred and selfish pretenses,
Threats of bullets and rattlings of guns and
cannons.

And I wonder where that little heirloom of joy
That I am heir to, is to be found.

A WORD FOR MY FATHER.

I was born in a village
Between the sea on the right
And to the left, near two rivers,
Bamboo groves, hills and wild flowers.

My father was one of those who dared to dig in there
first.
However beautiful the place was,
It ran wild with spooky tales and weird bushes
Tales of witchery, ghosts and eerie noises at night.

They say that once
Run away slaves were caught and brought back there.
It was sad.
No one knows what happened to them.
History had ceased to be written after that.

There were still places, in the bamboo clumps
Where weird arrangements of stones,
Lay still under wet coats of dark green moss
Like unfinished and abandoned graves.

Strange flowers grew in the humid shadows
Found nowhere else in the country,
Hibiscus and crocus that returned every April.
These still find their way into my poetry.

The old villagers called that place, Floreal,
The home of flowers.
A lovely name but a paradox too.
With the passing of the old thinking and traditions
Much had disappeared of the solid values.

Friendship is loose today and unpredictable,
And selfishness and greed
Carry shining faces.

From my father I learnt
That good and evil follow us beyond the grave,
Our inseparable companions.
For the venom that we serve others
always returns to us.

Enjoy the sunshine while you may,
He once said to me.
It is your rightful share of God's blessings.
Of all things, the holiest is this earth that we
live
And grow up on.
Be thankful for the harvests.

44

SIX   O'CLOCK.

Six o'clock.
All is serene and profound.
The last goat is back into the fold.
The sea has come to lounge on to the warm shore.

Like the white dove,
A wondrous sight of thorough peace has descended
On the belts of shredded casuarinas and the village.

Rocks and trees
Water and breeze
Bushes, hills and mountains, all adrift, drifting,
Drifting into the arms of a slumbrous dream world.

It was like a picture of receding hues,
A warring riot of colours.
The temple vesper's have sounded,
A silver clarion of small tinkling bells.
What a beautiful world!

I dearly yearn to reach out to this divine
peacefulness.
But I cannot, I fall half way.
My heart throbs, nervous.
My mind revolts, wild and uneasy.
My eyes prick and burn.

I sit on the shore, all alone,
Ruminating,
Full of fears, tears and uncertainties,
Rolling sounds of cannon thuds haunting my ears.
Somewhere in this miserable world tears are flowing.

I ask myself why is it all happening?
There is no lack of wealth in nature's purse,
I tell myself.
This world is big enough to wrap us all up in her
arms.

So much to be enjoyed freely and be happy about.
And yet in my heart, I am not at peace.
The evening pines.

This is a strange world,
Here the reapers are not always the growers.
Flower tubs spawn killer bullets,
And power is an opiating addiction.

The weight is getting too much,
The world is sagging
And tilting...

Stop a moment,
Shed no more tears.
Save some for the future...
If there is going to be a future!

One day the water will be soiled,
The flowers will go,
The sun will be harsher.
The hills, the mountains and the woodlands will dry
and die.
There will be no you
Nor me.

No vanity
No holy place painted with gold and fabricated
liturgies.
No manipulated faith.
Power will not buy a special place
In the endless firmament of God's grace.

There will be silence,
Clean unfinishable silence!
Primordial love

And virgin belts of peace.

Will man ever know man?

46

 BUSHES OF OLD GIRLS.

They are prickly and thorny,
Vicious
And virulently dark green.

But their flower stems, of all colours like delicate
little fingers
In clusters of yellow, red, white
Mixed yellow and red blooms.

I love them for the forbidden silence
That surrounds them
And the bees they attract.

I often wonder at the amount of honeyed sweetness
That is lodged in their hearts
That spins the bees in frenzy in the pleasant
sunshine.
They are wrong who say that evil comes from the
heart.

So I did not hate them, even when I was a child.
Never!
It is a breath of wisdom told by nature.

On my adventures in the village woodland,

I did get scarred though
And scratched, but I did not cease, like bees
To sip honey from the hearts of their dazzling
colours.

I used to enjoy this name too,
Old girls.
A bit hurting though,
As old unmarried women in the village were called
old girls.

Not all of them were prickly
Or forbidding,
They chatted and giggled round the village well
And turned the children's games and laughs into
electric pastimes.

At weddings,
No inhibitions, no problems,
The first to cackle off with jolly laughters,
Bare foot, skirts trussed up, dancing,
Flouncing on a drop of neat rum, they were marvels!

Eyes glinting and filled with fun,
Like the water of translucent streams,
They blazed with clean sincerity and abundance,
The first to start the carnivals, balls and jigging.
No one else dared!

They were not prickly either,
I thoroughly enjoyed the noise,
The songs and tambourines,
The wildness in their dances and movements.

I wonder now ,
Why like the other village girls they did not settle
down.
That was the tragedy.

So much love,
Sheer bubbling sincerity and gaiety,
Halos of infinite friendliness gone to waste.
Not a trace of pricks and pins like the wild bushes,
And yet they failed to attract lasting friendship.

The mistakes were not in their beautiful sense of
freedom,
Their sincere friendship
Or open heartiness,
But in the freakish judgement of the village elders,
Whose price for their empty ridiculous vanity,
The old girls paid.

48

BOOK OF LIFE.

The mind is like the ocean.
We are in it but still nowhere in it.
Life after life we come to its shores
And enjoy the sunrises and deplore the sunsets.

Still every time it is new.
Sometimes perchance, we know where we are.
At other times mostly we do not.

It is the same beautiful world,

Glorious with panoplies of blooms and smiles
Hills and mountains and lovely people,
Wondrous festivals at night as stars
Blaze forth their endless tinsels of lights.

We sit on these shores and watch the waves and the
billows
Rise and fume,
Playing with our thoughts and desires
Hardly knowing which way to spin them.

We wait for the sun to rise and the suffering to
end,
For tomorrow's sun to heal the scars of endless
waiting.
Only God knows what kind of catch will it be,
Meagre or rich!

How sweet, a new baby is born!
How devastating someone has to close his book
And make the way home across areas of infinite
nothingness
We smile a little.
We cry a lot!

But the way is the same for all of us.
Laugh if you can
Or cry,
But the writing goes on, in the light
Or in the dark.

Page after page,
Our own hands write the records of our destinies.
God watches, helpless.
We live by our will.

How could he interfere with what we ourselves
willingly write?
The words are our own,
The choice of directions and the goals
And the finished book.
The elation and the heartbreaks too,
Right or wrong!

Now and then between areas of long years,
To reprieve
God comes down to show us the way to end our
deviations.

Blessed are they who listen, and act on his advice,
For there shall be no more tears.

50

KEEP YOUR SMILES.

Heartbroken I stop at the feet of the old man,
Reticent and wise,
Face dark, sunburnt and windswept.

Says he in his usual tone,
Serene and deep, the way the man who knows speaks.
Wisdom he once said, does not reside on the tongue.
It is the fragrance of the flower sprouting from age
long seeds

Sown into a devoted heart.

Look at the sea, son
It is never at rest, sometimes blissful,
Then depressed and fuming,
Intent on destruction.

It goes up and high, violent, a killer.
It rushes, it crashes, it destroys,
Unconcerned, but foolish.

It takes nothing home.
The rest is flotsam, left for ever to float who
knows where?
If only it could learn that only peace begets peace
Only smile follows smile,
They die by bullets who worship bullets!

On those waves, son, is written the story of my
life,
My loneliness,
My search for fish and wisdom

Now and then I watch them chafing.
And I wonder whether I would ever return home,
My open skiff, frail and battered.

No one who lives on those waves,
Knows if the sun will ever rise for him again.
Many a time have I seen the stare of the grim
reaper,
Stark and ruthless, seemed to say time's up.

I smile back and say, as long as there is faith in
my heart
And my mind, strong and steady, I will pass you by,
my friend.
I will see the sun rise
I will catch the tail of the elusive tomorrow.

A song on my lips,
Faith in my heart
And strength in my arms,
I guide my boat back home to the shore,
For I know that somewhere
There is someone stronger than death.

The skiff is this frail frame, son and the
tumultuous ocean, life,
Mind and faith, my way and my will.
As sea cannot be without water nor trees without
leaves
Flowers and fruits,
Life is life because of its smiles and thorns.
Have faith, the sun will surely rise in the morning.

52

LET LIFE LIVE.

Many a night has passed by
And stars have come and gone.
No one cares any more.
There is a weird terror in the air.

Flowers have bloomed and waned.
Sunrises have emptied their harvests of colours

Into the unconcerned oceans.
Humanity is in a turmoil,
Caught into a maelstrom of uncertain future.
And death has never been a better scythe wielder
before.

The fear continues
And the uncertainty too.
We are all being stalked by a ghostly thing.

There is life being secretly snatched by the
ruthless enemy,
Bred and fed from into ourselves.
There is life being brutally cut short by insane
killers.
Killing has become a bit like shuffling cards.

Crazy armies stand facing each other,
Ready for indiscriminate slaughter.
Power drunk politicians think they have spare lives
to sacrifice.
No guilty feeling.
No compunction!

These are the people who in time of peace, sleep
soundly
In the glory of blood soaked pages of written
history.
Life is sacrosanct.
And nothing is greater.

Look around,
See the infinite wonders that God created in order
to preserve life.
To raise them, see the love he imbues into them.
What we cannot make ourselves
We have no right to destroy.

God is not attracted to your gold and gimmicks,
Displays of empty prayers, massive and gaudy
edifices
But by sincerity
Love and purity.

He finds God who sits quiet
Or with a flower
A fruit
Or a leaf,
In his heart, sincerely offering himself to him.

Everything belongs to him
Made by him
And given
To you and to me by him.

Today man has become the hunted,
Destiny the hunter,
Man the wriggly grub,
Destiny the vulture.

54

HOW BEAUTIFUL IS THIS NIGHT!

When the wind has finally rested,

Night blooms slowly from the bud of the parting day.
She opens her petals of mellow darkness,
A subtle and rolling display of dark haze
Studded with serene stars.

The village slumbers.
My eyes rejoice in their freedom from sleep.
For a while alive and thrilled,
I watch that wondrous opiating peace emerging.

Like a timid pigeon at first
It grows wings and gently flies to the many a
fantasy land
Of dreams and make-believe.

For not all nights are stalked by nightmares
And street terrors.
Not all nights rattle with murderous terror of
machine guns
And sniping bullets,
And thirst for blood.

There are still in this wonderful artifact of God
Many a thing of surpassing beauty.
Some may have lost faith and stood dazed
Others, faith in their hearts, trot on with a smile
on their lips.

So I leave my mind to loiter,
To wander amongst the multifarious wonders
Of nightly thrills,
Tender breeze, changes of colours in the sky
And hosts of drunken fireflies and the stars.

You sleep and you do not see them.
You do not hear them:
The ceaseless buzzing of the cicadas
The howls of a stray dog,

The sounds of the breeze in the trees.
You do not see behind the closed door,
That halo of light of the oil lamp burning.

And when the night is clear,
Boats of star lights sailing across the sky,
Or a hungry bat staggering eerily in the midnight
coolness.

Then the rarest of all sights, the spirit of the
night,
Running flashes of light snaking crazily
In the dry, remote and emblazoned emptiness.

Like thousand little burning wicks,
They wander in the cloudless sky.
Like thousands little bells, they tinkle in my
heart.

Like the chants of silence, the eternal sound,
Bubbling up waves after waves of creations
The inexhaustible fount.

They reach close to your heart and hug you
And you ask yourself why your eyes are wet.
These are real,
Not made up dramas.
It is the night, gently sweeping pass,
A woman's broad pall scattered with stars.

When you are in the opiating embrace of sleep

That takes you to the heart of the dream worlds,
You change reality for fantasy,
It is not the same when you wake up!

Humanity,
Nature sleep, how innocent!
How beautiful!
But how fake!

Wise men do not sleep.
They stay awake,
Eyes closed, peaceful, they wait.
They wait for the blissful showers of wisdom to rain
down,
The finer language of the night.

56

THERE IS A WAY OUT.

Lockdown
I shall stay at home till you tell me
I am safe.
It is not a big deal.
It is for my good.

I have very diligently listened,
Like a good child.
I have washed my hands many times a day,
Sometimes out of terror.
My nights screech with nightmares.
Eerily I see my hands foaming down the drain.

Have you ever fancied living in a tuna tin,
Cabined and cribbed?
My mind has turned into an inventory of items,
Thrown about in the house.
And as they screen, they turn me upside down all
night.

Still it is good to know where
My cans of beer and bottles of Grants are,
And the Courvoisseur and the red wines!
It is all for my own good!

Hold on, the holidays are not going to be back soon
though!
And I must do something to keep my mind sane.
A body without a sane mind is more dangerous
Than a mind without a sane body.

So, I shall fix my old bathtub in the back garden,
Let the water warm up in the English sun,
Add a handful of salt to give it a taste of the sea.

And to top it up, switch the fan on to run the waves
And the billows.
Let the flamenco start.
Ole!

Oh yes a couple of cans of Stella Artoise
Or Tennant,
That's not Spanish, I know
But they add to the colour and my taste!
Ho la la!

Well, of course
If it's not enough,
I can always order on line a couple of nicely
battered chicken
Legs
And chips.

For a day or two I'll forget about washing my
fingers.
I'll lick them!
This is my recipe for a fantastic lockdown.
Oh sorry, I forgot it's winter here!

THE MYSTIC SOUNDS

Often as I sit
My back to the silver-leaf tree,
And letting the silent chanting
Of the evening sea lull me to a quiet,
Leaving the robust world behind,
My eyes quiver to a peaceful rest.

And another world is born,
Teeming with new imageries and new sounds.
I hear strange and unknown music in my ears;
Sounds of harps and flute;
Of ceaseless choirs of birds and church bells.

Smaller bells tinkling,
Vying with one another
A symphony mellow, sweet and inebriating
Rising from places far beyond my understanding.

And when in my mind, the peace deepens,
At the back of my head

Rise a roar of the ocean and a roll of harmless
thunder.

Then, the most spectacular of wisdom pall
The sounds of running water,
Gradually easing the breath to a mystic stop.

Death comes and death goes,
Leaving me unbruised,
Drenched in the mellifluous arms of an ecstatic
peace.

Round holy fires
Hoary sages chant strange songs of wisdom
That tell of the eternal truth.

58

THE SHEPHERD AND THE VILLAGE WOODLAND.

When I was a child,
Strolling down my village woodland
A world of reality and of fantasy, flowers
And rowdy streams and little perils, was an
addiction.

A place that at once thrilled and awed me,
As I gazed down from the top of the slope
Towards endless sprawling valleys.

I whimpered in terror at the sight of those spooky
groves
Of bamboos, hollow and damp like haunted tunnels.
They squealed and whined, swayed and roared in the
winds,
A place of fearsome memories,
Untouchable at night.

There was then that wise looking shepherd.
Think of an extraordinary figure loitering about the
bushes,
His stick across his shoulders, his face rough and
deeply sunburnt.

A head scarf negligently sheltering his face from
the sun,
Followed by a herd of white goats
And you have him, the spirit of the woodland,
An indelible part of a throbbing mosaic.

Now forty years later,
He is still inspiring my poetry,
Him and his flock are still vivifying lines of my
writing.

At the sounds of his flute,
The hills exploded into an unsurpassable gaiety.
Passing birds, stunned, responded in beautiful
choirs,
Wayward streams flowed in awe, silent
And lightness eased the stifling heat.

He was part of a pleasant landscape
Embellished with hills, clear sky and mountains,
Colours of the sun set and fast shifting clouds
And those haunting plaints of pigeons, crazily in
love.

The end of the day could find him anywhere,
Dozing on the ground, his goats chewing the cud
near-by
Or near the old cemetery at the foot of the hill.
Even like the old
Pan sitting on the top of one of the huge rocks
On the river bank.

He was a piece on the mantel shelf of the woodland
That changed not as to where things were,
But as to where he was.

60

FROM DARKNESS LEAD ME TO LIGHT

Like the breeze,
Chasing sheaves of sunshine on the sugar cane
fields,
Like the vagrant fragrance of the reticent queen-of-
the-night,
My mind yearns to be free,
To rise above those threads of desires
That hold man prisoner to ignorance.

This world was made to free me.
I have turned it into a halter,

Confinement, and prison bars, I am bound,
A willing prisoner to the mind and the five rowdy
horses.

For He who made this sacrosanct place
Said that the labour and the fruits shall be mine to
enjoy.
The flowers shall be mine, the hills and the
mountains,

The clear sky and the moonlit nights, full of gentle
stars,
The fertile fields and the seas.
There will rough winds too
And thunder clouds,
Ocean storms and floods, think not of them as
enemies.

For he vanquishes who lives with the quiet
And the storm,
The flowers and the thorns.
Enjoy my munificence, he said but seek not to
possess it.
There lies the pain.
It is as elusive and impermanent as the fleeting
will-o-the-wisp.

Wisdom lies in wise choosing.
Make of your will and endurance, your armour and
shield
And of your sword, the sword of destiny.
For with your suffering, your joys and tears,
You write your own destiny.

When your mind is quiet
And your heart full of love
Learn then to combine the gifts
Like in a concoction brew and watch wonders arise.

Thunderstorm will turn into rain and rain into life
and plenty.
From your heart, wisdom long buried
Since time began its crazy race, will speak to you
In unsylabled silence.

Time has changed.
So has humanity.
Led by temptation to possess and greed
A slave to the senses, man has forgotten the purpose
Of his visit to this wondrous place.

Wisdom has waned, cold darkness rejoices in his mind
Bound by ruthless and uncanny beliefs
And hostile conducts
He has made of himself a rodent,
Shamelessly feeding on what others have laboured.

The way back is dark
And risky.
My nights rumble with rattling of machine guns
And raucous laughters of flying bullets,
Crying of unwanted children and abused women.
This was not what He who gave me those gifts made.

Maybe somewhere
In the depth of my being I can still find peace
And the joys I left behind.

He thought he chose the right place to live in my
heart.

From the innocence of a virgin land,
I have made of it the lands of angry boars.

62

SETTING   THE   MIND   FREE.

This place has far more things in it
Than you and I
Can ever cognise.

Still,
Cloistered
In our minds
We are happy to live in a mental bunghole.
Just round the village,
Or safe within the confines of our inhibitions.
The rest is seemingly false and dangerous.

Some like it this way,
Slaves to short-lived glitters and baubles,
Terrified by what lies beyond the familiar fringes.
The search for themselves has yet to begin.

When you tell them
This is light,
They tell you it is superstitions,
Darkness and perdition.

The radiance and the glory of this universe
Reside in its ceaseless flux
Embellished with frills of wisdom,
Happiness, beauty, love and truth,

Changes guarantees the continuous existence of life.
It is not a child's play.

In there,
In the lotus of transcendental serenity,
Where you
And I wait
For the realised consciousness to emerge,
Immortality is not a fiction.
It is a lasting reality.

Nature changes,
Trees and mountains change,
Sceneries change
And so do stars.

Brooks become streams
And streams rivers;
Rivers become seas
And seas oceans, all moving towards the immortal
truth

Here
The mind dreams of its own lost splendour,
A consciousness that knows
No fear, no bound.

Cloistered behind bars of false values,
and sparse light
And stale air,

The mind recycles itself on destructive rags and
tatters,
And finally explodes into heartlessness and
bloodshed.

Thus, God makes wisdom
We make nightmares.
God makes peace
We make terror.

God makes beauty
We make the beast
And turn this beautiful place into a place of smog
And hatred.

64

FOR THE TWO OF YOU

When one day I am gone
Pass the beautiful ways of the stars
The flowers
And the seas,
Do not be too sad or grieve for me.
I have lived my life and made it a little better
Than what God gave me.

I have grown many flowers in my garden.
But I never gave them to Him.
I only offer Him those that I grow in my heart.

Think then that everybody takes the same way back.

He who comes to this world must one day leave it.
This is not a fool's paradise, that life is for
ever.
Only the Spirit is immortal and moves to another
sheath
When the time comes, on its way to its
transcendental abode.

Some have loved me.
Others have hated me.
Still others have not cared.

I pray for them but I cannot shoulder
The load of their wrong doings, it is theirs.
No amount of forgiving will free them from the
fruits
Of their actions.

For those who hate, and who cause others to shed
tears,
Little know what they do.
We are free to do what we want.
Still one day the consequences of our actions
Will catch up with us, it will be a sad day then.

Destiny is a ruthless and dedicated debt collector.
You harvest what you sow,
Subtly, the consequences of our actions catch up
with us.

Some fools say that they did not ask to be born
again

Yes they did.
Or even choose the family they are born in
Yes they did

We always come back to collect the rewards of our
good actions
Or pay for the wrong ones
At the right place and at the right time.
Health and happiness follow good actions.
Always!
Help ever
Love ever
Hate never.

Though we are far apart
Me in the north
And you in the South
What a marvel, but what does it matter?
Destiny is the eternal link.

66

THIS PLACE IS MY PLACE OF LABOUR.

Little I know the place I came to
And on whose door to knock.
Little I know the way that leads to heaven
Or to hell!

There are flowers around
And the hills and the mountains are beautiful,
Wondrous and touching.

And there are gales and storms.
There are wilderness
And the tears of the poor are plentiful.
Blood still flows from the cross of each of us.

Now and then in the silence of the night
I can hear the loud guffaws of rattling guns,
And raucous laughters of explosions!
Little I know the place I came to.

Still something in me uncannily says,
I know this place, dear to me now
Dear to me always
The same that inside me secretly send waves of
peace.

Make of it whatever you want.
Grow hate and divisions
Sow bullets,
It is not your place,
Nor mine.

One day from the ether,
Floods and earthquakes, gales and storms will come
down
And write down the history of the wrong doings
You left behind.

But for me I will not cease to run seas and oceans
Of love and gaiety.
One day we will certainly reap the fruits of our
labour!

TUNA   SANDWICH.

When next you go to hell
Please make sure you come and tell.

Nothing is new here
Not that very dear.
Except an enemy is on the rampage
And death is making a mockery of our lives.

Even the need is not there to go to hell.
It is here!
I love the trees and the sun,
I love my homily river
And the insane flights of the wandering bees.
Sadly I am made to miss the fun.

Days going by, dreary and interminable
Eyes tired with tv watching
Eating tuna sandwich and beer drinking.

I never wanted to be a cloistered priest.
For oh I love to wander amongst the trees
And watch the sea rise and fall,
Ceaselessly playing its hoary tricks.

I love to lose myself in the crowded village
markets.
I would sneak into the children's games round the
well
And listen to the songs of the wandering minstrels.

I miss those pleasures,
Those long walks full of freedom.
How hard I need to be on my heart
That is dying to reach out to the wandering clouds

And the continuous vaunting of the birds flying
above.
They are free.

GLORY TO THEE OH MIND

Blaze, mind,
Blaze forth your radiance!

Some day in the future,
Our mortal tryst will end
And I will then witness your ineffable resplendence.

Not this vagrant instrument of fake and relative
attractions,
fear and short lived joys.
I will see the same
That was never seen by me, your primal glory...

Not till this soul has risen to its cosmic bonfire
of self-realization.
Resting at last in the mellow sweetness of
tranquility
Merged into the serene lake of meditation.

Heretofore, slave to the restless senses,
You made a slave of me too,
Ignorant of my true identity.

I followed, blind
Leaving behind eternal heritage of happiness

For the valleys of temporal pleasures.

Little I realise
That I exist in a ceaseless flux,
A transfiguration,
A prisoner to pain and pleasure in areas of
ceaseless uneasiness,

A mere shadow,
Now here
Then nowhere, that made of me
A fated moth
In the web of mortality.

Still,
However insatiable and indomitable
You are
However much you made me
Run,

However unbearable the pain I suffered at your hands
I hail you as my master.
Blaze forth your primordial effulgence, oh mind!
I needed to taste the fruits of bitter tears,
Reactions to my own actions.

I needed
To understand the depth of this creation
Hidden behind a facade of perpetual movement,
I need to slow down this vertiginous speed
That hides the reality.

In order to taste undiluted wisdom
I wandered in delusion, created by you.
Then through my serenity,
I could see the glory of my own immortality.

You it was who made me weak,
To realise my strength,
To know that I can, like the mythical Phoenix
Rise again from the ash of my despair.

You it was who taught me
That pain and hopelessness
Are strength in disguised,
And initiated me into the secrets of calm
equilibrium,
Non-attachment.

70

And that when on my journey, surrounded by delusions
Confused,
And darkness abound,
You it was
Who taught me to seek inside this heart
For my very own light.

Glory to thee, oh great teacher,
Glory to thee!

A TOUCH OF WISDOM.

Poetry is not just lining up words,
Closet them within sets of rules
And spin them out to cry and die.

Words are not dead sticks.
They have Souls
And they have more strength than we can think of.

They are the keepers of our deepest secrets,
Joys, laughters and sadness, restlessness
Wonders and inspirations too.

In times of sadness
They are the unseen tears that rise in the heart.
In joy, the concealed rivers of subtle and fine
feelings.

There is no beauty in deliberate confinement.
Keep a bird in a cage,
And it dies a slow and miserable death.

For freedom is Word
And Word is Poetry.
Freedom is beauty, the very nature of the cosmic
Soul.

Poetry is the mergence of beauty and freedom,
That droops and dies when forgotten
Behind heartless prison bars of the fickle mind.

Poetry is flower alive,

Swaying in the breeze and wind
Poetry is the silence on the evening shore
And the inspirations of the ripples.

72

The wind that sweeps the dusty roads of the village
Into furls of dancing wonders,
The flamboyant in conflagrations,
The village well where women chatter
And children play.

Where dusts, hibiscus and tender morning sunshine
Merge to play the ancient games of the simple
everyday life,
Where the ox cart steel wheels crunch on the brittle
road.
This is Word in action
And Poetry blooms.

For life is free.
Oh set me free too,
Free from the confinements of books,
And religions and hypocrisy,
They have made a willing slave of me.

Let me wander in the subtle labyrinths of life,
Lost but wise
And myself.
Let my mind rise to the beauty of the hills
And mountains.

Let me merge into the joys of the gregarious bees.
Let me like the fireflies dance in the dark
And die to rise into a Phoenix of eternal light.

I shall be here my friend, when you return
To seek the ever lasting freedom in poetry.
My words will echo from the antiquated pages of
time.

I shall be here to tie the knot of love,
The love that you knew and lost,
The love that transcends books and holy places.

The same that makes the sun rise
And set
And gives gentle fire to the stars.

We shall, in a new bouquet of the starry moonlit
nights
And the immortal fragrance of the queen-of-the-
night,
Welcome the love that never died
Written in the immortal language of unsylabled
poetry.

74

THE MAN   AND   HIS   VIOLIN.

That man, he plays the violin
At the end of my road.
No shelter for his white haired head,
Rain washed, sun burnt,
Eyes sunken and haggard, a lone figure.

Like a radiant sun behind a still veil of darkness
His face shines with patience and a mystic smile.
He does not bother whether as you pass-by
You ring his bowl with a coin.

He does not ask to know how big the world is,
Nor how small is his town.
Every now and then, a piece of newspaper passes him
by
Driven desultorily by the wind.

It does not stop.
It does not toss a coin into his bowl either.
It flies pass wild, buzzing non-stop
A flighty language, conflagrating with spits and
venom.

At the end of the day,
When with weakness and pain, the knotty hands shake,
Tears in his old eyes, his chest cramped,
The violin squeaks and shivers, uncertain,
He lays down his instrument and picks his bowl.

Empty!
And yet the whole world has passed by.
The mystic smiles broadens,
Stronger, braver and more illuminating.
A smile of resolution not to lose,
To live above the ash and play on.

Life is a whirlpool, no one can tell
What comes from the churning of it,

He has taught himself.
The bowl is empty, that is his victory.

No heart break!
That is his freedom, his strength.
He is the master
Both of the music and his life.
He is the music, he is the violin
And he is the listener.

THE RIGHT WAY IS ALWAYS RIGHT.

Not many rivers flow to merge with the sea.
Not all flowers bloom to reach the altar of God.

Whipped by winds and storms,
Seared by the noonday heat, they wilt
Waiting for the coolness to be kinder and the
tomorrows
More uplifting and enlivening.

For many, tomorrow is a chimera,
Or a figment, a mere ideation, a day after a long
sleep,
An illusion in the mind of man,
It never comes.

Before the coming of the coolness,
The river dries,
The flowers wane.

It is not easy to know what will tomorrow bring.

Sources of joy to the heart,
One by one,
Like gentle snowflakes, the petals fall
Back into the arms of the loving mother,
That gave them birth.

Like the rivers and the streams, we loiter
Down the lanes of life in search of success
And happiness.

Blessed is he who finds eternal happiness in this
world.
Unhappy man can only chant of unhappiness.
World of living illusions can only ultimately
engender illusions
And tears.

76

Life is like grains of sands,
It is constantly slipping through the fingers.
Those are great Souls who having mastered
The laws of holding the grains of sands from
slipping.
Sit quiet and unbewildered,
 And wait.

One day perchance when we learn to stop
Counting the pages of our successes,
And broaden our visions of what this world is really
about
And what we ought to be busy about,

We will discover that reality has far more
dimensions to it
Than this fragile existence gives to our thoughts;
That our mind and heart have been hijacked
By the ignorance of our marauding senses.

That unknown to us
We have been going the wrong way all along;
It is more tedious to make a tread back now,
The burden is not the same as when we began.

The truth and the way to it are those relics of
wisdom
Many a wise man has sacrificed himself in order to
guide us.
We turn our backs on them for a brew of quick
success.
The rest is continuous pain, struggling in the net
of false hopes
And illusions.

SOMETIMES EVEN STONES SHED TEARS.

For no reason of mine
I see myself in the dark.

My room is dark with fear,
My children terrified.
What shall I tell them?

Other than a few frolics
And bike rides,
They barely know what life is,
How shall I explain it to them?

That we stand between here and nowhere.
The boat of life is rocking,
For them, for me
For everyone.

Who shall I tell not to put the light out?
The fear is alive, gnawing
Searing!
Devastating!
The enemy is stronger than us all.

Who cares when the stars come out
And when they go?
When the flowers bloom
And when they wane?

The moon is pale, cold and jaundiced.
Thunder clouds stand still.
Alone , isolated, behind the curtains,
I dare not look out.

I dare not listen
Why oh why?
Have we come so far, oh God
To be hurriedly dumped into crude and unholy holes?
Is humanity so cheap, of no value?
Not any more?

I can only survive till I can.
My candle will not last for ever either.
Soon the light will go
And darkness will prevail.

Darkness comes when light goes,
But Lord, light does not always come when darkness
leaves.
No sunrise will ever hail the parting of the dark
sky again.
For many, darkness and emptiness will always scream
When the doors are shut, and someone has been left
behind.

Fear will remain.
The wounds in the heart will continue to cry
The freshness of the air will never be the same.

Light is yours
And the eternal too.
But this little candle light in my room is mine,
Made from the tallow of my sweat
And blood
From my tears, my pain and losses.

This I offer at your altar,
Save my lonely room from going dark.
Let the light last
Let my faith and hope last.
Have mercy for our tears and suffering.

THE ROBIN.

I wake up to a gleaming carpet of snow
In my back garden and a cold shiver runs down my
neck.

Yet enthralled, my heart fights to feast
On the rich and flaky white canopy.
I stroll my eyes around.

The camellia, darker in the cold embrace,
Laden with more than its fair share,
Objects openly and gives a discontent shake
As a brisk breeze swoops down on it.

My heart warms up.
Life has not all come to a stop, I think.
For lo!
On the top of the frozen pansies.
There is a brisk movement.

Undaunted, a little robin is busily pecking,
Skipping, strutting as it challenges a mound of
snow.
It stops suddenly and peers down.

All frenzied, legs apart and wings wide open,
It begins to drill, deeper and deeper.
Victorious, it brings out the tiny morsel of a
wriggly worm.
Oh man, what a dance follows!

As if hearing my thoughts, it jumps up
And lands near my window, on a rose stem.
And sings, a gentle metallic sound:

I wonder how big is this world.
In shine and shower I dig for grubs.
But I am terrified at night though,
In my nest dangling at the top of a bush
When the wind blows and shakes.

And I cry in the morning
When I see my young ones dead on the ground.
In this small body,
There is a big heart that loves and desires love.

We are all the same, big or small, see.
Cry not for me, for I know what life is.
There is the flower and there is the thorn,
He is wise who lives happily with both.

THIS IS AS FAR AS WE GO.

I wander down the wood lanes
As the warm summer breeze gently breathes through my
hair
Whispering in my ears,

Words of wisdom, carried from hoary times

When the world glowed with pure light
And wise men sat quiet inside themselves
Searching for the meaning and the mysteries of
life.

Those same that transcended the spheres and the
space,
Life and death,
That today ceaselessly ring in my ears,
Tickling in vain my dormant mind.

Like the mountains and the dull hills
Ignorant, I sleep,
A slumber of ignorance.

How strange is this cosmic arrangement.
We are like kites,
Stringed to the will of the maker
But free,

Free to play in the gentle breeze,
And dare dark thunder clouds and the storms.
Still when all is said and done,
We can only go as far as our string goes,
No further.

And if we do
God only knows where we could end.....
Those buried civilizations are witnesses to our
digressions.

WHERE CAN I FIND HIM.

Night and day
Your names continue to echo in my heart
And Your image fill my mind's eye.

I seek Thee far and wide,
In my tears
And in my smiles, everywhere.
And yet I see thee not.

Still from the serene warmth of the valley's sunlit
shadows,
The breeze brings a waning strain of your flute.
Tears in my eyes
Sobs choking my heart, I loiter in vain.

Near the river,
Near the pond
Down the village slope,
No one has seen you.

The villagers laugh at my naivety
And ask if I have ever seen the wind,
Or the willow stop shedding tears.

I watch the flowers' ecstatic sways, like possessed
Fanning colours and fragrance.
They too dance to the tunes of your flute,
Naughty! naughty!
They say you are.

The will-o-the-wisp of the dusky evening sun,
The shimmers in the fleeting runs of the ripples on
the pond,
Teasing the heart is your favourite pastime.

The enchanting sounds of your flute
And your fleeting fragrance,
Caught in the starry spinning of the crazy nights
Are dear memories of rare encounters.

Oh how crazy of me!
I say to myself.
Why do I search for the unsearchable?
My suffering is my love.

Seeking is hollow.
I am Him, He is me.
There has never been a me
How can the fragrance be without the flower?
There is no river without water.

If I cannot catch the breeze
Nor the mystic fragrance of the rose,
If I cannot stop the ripples from dying on the
sunset shores
Nor catch the dance of fleeting shadows on the
hills,

How then can I catch the uncatchable,
He who has no frame nor form?
It is my love that gives him form.
I am like the musk deer, I die trying to find
What I carry in myself.

This is why the flowers

And the breeze are silent
The villagers and the hills are stunned.
For He is your own special and personal experience.

84

ODE TO THE CRAZY FIREFLIES.

Like a tender screen
The summer dark slowly furl down from the mountains.
No sound of footstep
No eerie tremour psych from the parting daylight.

As the village gradually eases into a slumber,
The tired and breathless breeze comes
To roost on the darkening woodland, trees cease to
strum,
Birds to fly.
I thrill to the possession of the entire night,
All to myself.

In the remote serenity of that vast space above,
A straggly handful of stars look down like silver
tinsels.
It is the world of tranquility, of dreams,
A time to unshackle oneself from the chains of daily
servility,
To surrender to the sweet inebriation of the restful
night.

But not so with the fireflies!
There is madness in the air,
There is exultation.
There is extravagance of endless dances,

There is music of unheard-of mystic enchantment.

See the dance in your mind's eye.
In your heart, hear the music.
If you are subtle enough,
You will see these transcendental dances.

You will be wrapped into waves after waves of cosmic
sounds,
Flute, gentle harp and choir of birds, and running
water
Tinkling of temple bells
And chimes of mighty church bells.

You will see the shivers of their translucent wings
As they flit round the street lights
And dance in utter abandonment.

However hard I spin my muse,
However broadly
I throw the nets of my words in that warm moonlit
air,
They return empty handed, a futile chase!

My heart still insatiated,
Drunk, exulting in those endless dreams of fast
dives
And plunges
And cheeky exuberance of slashes and dips.

They are fireflies, I tell myself,

Not me not you.
There is no world
There is no space, and there is no thinking
There is no failures
And there is no success.

There is only love
And the fire.
Only them and the endless musical motions
Into the infinite joys of self- immolation.

86

WILD LAUGHTERS

Strident laughters of guns in the dark
Lit a sinister bonfire in the night
As behind restless screens of flying dusts
The stars hid their faces.

Tucked behind a shattered mound of dusty clutters
Reeking of wet blood and bullets,
My eyes itched.

Across a pall of ugly darkness,
An area of bombarded stones,
Once a busy road,

A thriving market place
That rang with children's frolicsome laughter
And women's haggling,

There was a clatter of gunfire

And a shaded figure fell.

Was he dead?
Was he bleeding?
He groaned.
He moved.

And then,
There was a quiet,
Devastating
Eerie and cold.

Dry as a barren rock
My stomach heaved,
Hollow with fear.

Life has become a desperate animal
On the run,
To be torn apart,
At the mercy of heartless maulers.

As light finally dawned,
Above the knoll of stones,
My eyes rested
On the cold hand of that man
Pointing towards the heavens.

In a rage of despair
I laughed,
I cried
And I screeched.

Sometimes they say
Even love spawns scorpions.

If this is what life is all about,
Like a grounded lion
Hemmed round with a ring of ruthless fire,

Then glory lies
In facing the fire.

88

TO CARE OR NOT TO CARE.

Some say we live only once.
Great news!
With odd things going about these days,
Scare in my heart, I hail the proclamation!

Others say we will come back.
I am scared of the wisdom in here.
Still I wonder what side am I on?

Believe me,
I prefer to sit on the fence,
And let the philosophers, the journalists
Or the politicians sort it out.

Before your own eyes,
They could coldly cut you open alive,
Then with a cool dissembling balanced smile

Tell you there is nothing to worry.
Moron experts!

As a poet I love beauty and quietness.
Arguments bore me.
Catch the serenity behind the dawning evening
And surrounding the woodland, that profound
tranquility
That sneaks you on board to a world of everlasting
bliss.

I look behind all things,
Where unseen hands
Are continuously weaving endless tapestries of
miracles,
Where sounds have no sound
And what you see and feel come to you
On waves of wordless messages

See beauty in silence,
In the heart's beat, the hills and down the
mountains.
There is beauty in splashing in the countryside
stream,
And watching the light and translucent butterflies
Playing in breezy sunshine.

There is beauty in the lonely wild flowers
That deck the road sides.
Watch the inspired thrush singing
And the drunken black bird tyrolling.
They make my heart heave with bliss.

Why should I care whether I live
Or die?
Someone else needs to care about this.
I am sick of being donkey driven by circumstances
Or destinies!

Not all the ways lead to the ocean.
Heaven is in me, I hate to get lost in jungles of
words
And invented philosophies,
And fossilized liturgies.

So when my time comes,
I am ready, nicely packaged.
If I do not come back
The parting was well made.
But if I do, we will hopefully have a tot together.

90

SMILES AND TEARS.

Smile is life.
And life is holy, the munificence of the Lord.
True or not, it is the transcendental reason
For the flourish of this universe.

So when life thrives,
Flowers bloom,
Hills and mountains shiver with green exuberance,
Sounds of warbling fill the air,

Trees rejoice with weights of fruits.

Innocent, children play, thrill and laugh.
Fields explode with abundance
Humanity is as happy as God wants him to be.

There comes a time though, when this dream is
shattered
And the smile freezes into terror.
Aghast, humanity stand still,
Tears flow
And fears and wastelands claim the fields of human
life.

At night we pray for the sun of hope to rise,
To be free from nightmares and uncertainty,
Nights are sleepless.

From one room to the other, I tread
Drying the tears from the eyes of my children's
feverish sleep.
In despair I run out of comfort,
My arms full,
My heart cold and dry, I wrestle to keep my sanity.

I stand alone, the windows forbidden.
Eerie!
There is an enemy outside.
I can sense it,
But in the dark I cannot see him.
It smells of the grave, invisible and invincible.

In the dark the beautiful smile on my young
daughter's lips

Is like a sunrise,
It lights my heart
And I break into chants of courage
And hope.
I let myself go down on my knees
And pray.

No one lives for nothing.
And no one dies for nothing either.
This is not a cursed place,
Made from the subtle wheels of God's own spinner
hands
From where humanity once rose and grew up.

Where the wicked has to atone for their wrongdoing
And good is rewarded!
Where at dawn and dusk, vespers bless the cool
evening air;
From the desert to the towns
From the temple to the churches.

If God's willing, we will live.
The battle will stop,
The bloodshed will cease.

And again the smiles will light the valleys and the
hills
Ways will open!
Strength will again grace the majesty of this place,
We will certainly not run before the rage of this
evil.

Man will be man again,
The haven of the Creator's grace,
Not the hell he has made himself into.
Why seek hell elsewhere,
It takes a single step to find it inside some of us.

WHAT A WONDERFUL CREATION

Early at daybreak I chase the morning sun
And bathe in the flood of wandering mist.
I watch the sugar cane fields wave in the breeze,
And I thrill to the blithesomeness of the newborn
day.

I ask myself what more do I need to make myself
happy.
Stay quiet, there is a twitter in the bush,
A mother bird is feeding a lonesome young.
Is not this entrancing?

The hibiscus flashes in the shy shade,
Shameless in its glorious purple
Tempting a cheeky sparrow.
In this great living panoply of marvels,
My poet mind dares not rise to the wonder of it all.

The universe is a mosaic
Full, throbbing and alive.
Now caught in the splendour of million tinsels of
sun rays
Then merges in the dream of moonlit darkness and
starlight.

Like an unseen hand playing on an unknown instrument
Endless wonders rise and blossom,
A certain wand orchestrating,
And the play of beauty unfurl in silence.

Flowers and mountains rise.

Hills and valleys roll out.
Blue skies open like a mother's arms
And dark space rejoices in the crazy dazzle of
winking stars.

Who knows when
And where it all began,
A certain unfinishable symphony
Into which I merge myself.

Hold your pen poet!
On your knees,
On your knees, for your heart has no more room
To garner this cosmic explosions!
Where shall I put my next word?
The rest is silence.

94

A SORDID TRUTH OF LIFE.

It had poured all day,
Rancorous blasts of winds and rain,
When finally I arrived at the hospital.
My wife was in the last throes of a cancerous
nightmare.

She was never intended to come back home with me.
Long past midnight,
Tired, I left her bedside for a while.

Outside,
Soaked, lying on a drenched bench,
Her bare feet in the rain,
Her hair, loose and tangled,
Was a woman about forty, sleeping
A drunken and feverish slumber,
An empty bottle of mixed cider and beer on the
flloor!

Was that real?
I thought of my wife dying upstairs.
And I cried.
Not for my wife, but for that woman!

I have never hated anyone in my life,
But on that night, gripped by a massive attack of
sickness
Bitterness and revolt, I hated life, I hated
everyone,
I hated this bloody world and God for being so
heartless!

Here was a woman who wanted to die
But could not.
And my wife who wanted to live,
And could not.

BEAUTY THAT NEVER DIES.

I wonder what real beauty is.
Beauty that transcends the boundaries of this place
And never fades.

Beauty that exhilarates the groveling senses and
lift them
To pitches of divine inspirations.
Beauty that defies the battering of the weather
And the arrogance of Time.

I sing of the beauty of sunrise
And the golden daylight.
I thrill to the beauty of sunset
And the serene peacefulness of the village hills.

But they are there only for the day.
They vanish
And leave my heart cold, empty, hungry.

Why then does the day end?
Why does the sun set?
And the dark frightening?
Why do we all,
like the birds and beasts, hurry so frantically
home?

Why is the uncertainty in nature so agonizing
As darkness boldly braces its way in?
Why do my pain and fear linger
And the threats of terrifying nightmares deepen?

Where has all the love gone?
Why has man for a mere handful of tempting coins
Lost the sight of those beautiful and great visions
of wisdom,
Left behind by the great sacrifices of the
enlightened Ones?

The blooms have faded, the place is desolate,
The hills and the valleys sob in silence
The churlish breeze whines and eyes are full of
tears.

Look at the stars in the night sky, so many of them,
They do not fight each other!
This is the beauty I seek,
The peace and the love.
Why then do we sow the tempests?

I have nicely woven many dreams for you.
The most beautiful flowers,
Threaded with locks of colourful sunrise,
Where like children, hope and happiness play
In the sunshine of life, all for you.

Cease to grow bullet
They can only spawn flowers of hate and death.

SEEK THE REASON.

We do not always see the reasons beyond things.
We think there is none.
But reasons are there, profound and wiser

Than we realize..

Why things appear
And why they fade?
Why the tears and why the smiles?
Why the flower blooms, and why it wanes.
These are not mere discardable miracles!

Why there is wind
And why the breeze?
Why the torrid desert sun
And why the gentle village warmth?

We look at the frames of things
The superficial side
And decide
To hate or not to hate
To keep or not to keep
To love or not to love.

There is more than this frame can tell.
The beauty, the wisdom and the infinity
Lie beyond.

How poor in wisdom we are!
We come back to the same shore life after life,
Play with the same pebbles and walk the same ways,
Still remain blind to the ancient reality,
That waits to be uncovered.

We know the stars and the space,
Still we do not wonder why they are there.

We know the earth
And man, the hills and mountains
Birds and nature,
Still few are puzzled or wonder!

Like all things we come, ignorant
And we go back, ignorant.

There is a reason.
He is wise who sits quiet
And let his mind and heart drift
Beyond the narrow precincts of mortal limitations.

TEARS OF A POET.

I will fill the hearts of those who are deprived of
hope.
I will light smiles on the lips of those who are
alone,
Whose nights scream with nightmares of pains and
tears.
For I have known all of them,
My words shed the same tears.

And when darkness has vanished,
All eyes blaze forth the exuberance of this blessed
creation,
I shall sit on my bed of simple straw,
Amongst the stars and the serene moonlight,
Spin endless strains of hope and faith in the
Creator.

How strange are the fireflies, drunk in their dreams
of light,
Love and sacrifice
And surrender,
Self-immolation into the eternal glory of light!

I shall on my old banjo, string soft notes of music
To the festivals of twinkling lights in the dark
sky,
And let the dreams pass by.
For who knows of what stuff is dream made of ?

Not all dreams are dreams I want to dream.
Some scare, others terrify,
And leave my brows with unwanted bath of hot sweat.

Life is not equal to every one.
Some get less
Others more.
Some get trials and tribulations,
Others skids through with ease.
We are surrounded with mysteries, ready to be
unraveled.

Perchance in this life, I shall find my dream.
It will be my dream,
The one I spin with love in my heart,
Full of strength and peace.

100

One that will rise from the ash of all my pain and
despair,
My own,

My very own.
Perchance then, back into that dream
I shall make everybody's dream whole.

FRIENDS.

When we speak of friends,
Sadly I always feel a cold shudder racing down my
back.
Far and wide have I wandered,
Dared rough areas, towns and cities,
Seeking a friend who is honest.

Friends have come and friends have gone.
Like sugar attracting marauding ants,
They enjoyed the fruits of my labour,
Nears and dears, selfish and hungry.
Steady as long as the bottle of rum runs
And the table is full.

Who cares that my boat is gone,
Carried one night by rough seas?
No more fish to grace the table,
No more friends either.
Old age and sickness have come to stay
And my bones rattle with pain.

The old bottle of rum has long ago disappeared,
Buried into the sand of time.
The evenings no longer ring

With the usual sounds of the triangles and the
tambourines
And no songs hit the moonlit nights.

Why are the tambourines silent?
The casuarinas are still green and robust,
Commanding the sea,
The Conde birds yodeling.
But the grass is quiet, no echo of approaching
footsteps.

102

In this star lit tranquility,
A presence of serene comfort and hope still lingers.
The last flower that dares to grace my wasteland,
The last song that enlivens the parched desert of
my life.
And I realise,
Dear dear Friend, that there is only you remain
behind.

TO HELL WITH HELL.

Now and then I wonder why man loves
To create hell for himself?
Dark moods and jealousy
Words that hurt, lies and fabrications

Hypocrisy and heartlessness and selfishness,
Are the robust fibres that strengthen the hell in
us.

Man has more than his fair share of suffering in
this world,
Why then is he bent on creating another hell?
Why then does he prepare another bed of nails?

This world thrills with fake gods and dodgy truths,
That can be bought and sold for a penny
Down the market place.
Some scream for our blood,
The others, by diverse subtle ploys,
Turn our nights into nightmares.

They pamper our gullibility and knead our vanity
How passionately they tear the true saints
And the holy men
And set fire to the brittle firewood of our
spiritual ignorance.

We are not afraid to hurt any more,
We are not afraid to kill.
We gladly enjoy the harvests of another man's
digging.

Many a holy man will pass this way, dear friend.
Blinded by our search for hell
And vanity and fake spirituality,
Few amongst us will ever spot him.

I finally found a way to be free from all these webs
And unwanted prison bars,
I let hell go to hell,
I live the way I love!

WHEN THE DAY I S DONE.

When the day is done
And my herd of goats and sheep are in their folds,
When the woodland is quiet
And the remote light of a rising moon crowns
The heads of the hills.

I sit quietly by a fire of sticks and dry leaves
And ruminate on the days gone by.
Like everything, time came
And time went.

I have nothing,
Except for a little love in my heart
And a smile on my lips,
I have never had anything and I am happy.

What do I care what happiness is
Or maybe heartbreaks?
They are frequent visitors, like lost souls,
I let them pass by.
For this beautiful world does not belong to me alone

I love the village that gave me birth
And the well.
I love the flowers, always in bloom
The hills and the mountains that never ask for
anything
For the infinite pleasures they give me.

I love the sea that lulls me to sleep in the
distance
And the strident screeches of the gulls that wake me
up

The ceaseless whistling of the breeze
In the ragged casuarinas.

I love the little children
I greet on the way to the hills
And the wildness of the hibiscus sweeping down
The slopes in those rare ecstasies of purple blooms.

That sunburnt make-shift cremation ground
Berthed in a spindly eucalyptus belt,
It always reminds me that there is always an end to
everything.

That the tragedy is not in ending there
For this is inevitably the fate of all things:
The soul needs to renew itself.
The pain is in setting roots to a place
That was never intended to be ours.

106

AND LIFE IS A MYSTRY.

Sometimes on my way
I meet with thorns,
And sometimes flowers.

Sometimes on my way
I meet with tears

And sometimes smiles.
In the fields of life, thorns and flowers
Tears and smiles grow wild and side by side.

To avoid the agony of some,
I pretend they are not there,
That the flesh is not lacerated, that the smile will
last for ever.
I turn to prayer and to my will,
To nights of tearful loneliness, to drink and to
drug.

Seized into a river of no return, flowing, flowing.
This body is always losing.
I cry, but the heartbreaks stay.
I laugh but the sun makes a rapid plunge.

I have often wondered what life is all about!
Is it a mystery, a motivation
Or a transcendental game of dice?
Neither you nor I know.
You can eliminate this frame, but not the spirit.

In my old age this frame still bears
The scars of the old whippings of time,
Dull eyes and restricted movements.

They had long thinned out those little moments of
joy
That I had.
Wise men say the flowers are my very own growing
And the thorns too.

The pain is my very own creation
And the joys too.

In my keenness to be ahead of life,
I have become a victim to the old memories.
Some come back to soothe my broken heart,
Others return to haunt me.

Yet I believe the sun will rise again tomorrow.
He is wise who welcomes pain and pleasure
With the same serene equanimity.
Some day, from somewhere good times will return.
This mystery will be revealed.

For whoever made us,
Surely did not intend us to be a toy to please
himself.

108

THE   SOUND.

In the silence of the night as I sit quiet
I hear the sound of a hum.

In the noises of the thriving day
It thrums award , unperturbed,
A quiet, infinite murmur
Trailing behind, the ecstatic beauty of a serene
mellowness.

At sunrise, drenched in the glow of golden rays,
From flowers in bloom
It rises,
And the scented breeze flows.

Nature thrills.

And at sunset,
As the sea ebbs and the hills slumbers in peace
And birds sail home,
It rises home to the infinite sky
The space explodes into an ineffable display of
stars.

For ever here
For ever there
In me
In you.

In the crazy falls of cascades,
In the woodland lake,
Down the valleys and up the hills
And mountains, everywhere!

It haunts like an endless symphony.
It blows like conches.
It rings like the vesper's bells.

It roars like the ocean,
And rolls like fearsome thunder.
No beginning and no end,
It creates and it dissolves
The same humming murmur, as old as the creation!

Where am I looking for it, dear friend?

It is in me,
It makes me,
It unmakes me.

A celebration of my own eternal spirit,
The transcendental umbilical cord that binds me
To the Eternity.

110

SING A SONG FOR ME.

That day I cried.
It was my birthday, an old man's scare!
And there was no one to sing a song for me.
Of all things, I yearned for a song.

The loneliness did not scare me,
Nor the silence of the nights.
I am used to them.

In my loneliness, sometimes I wanted to know
That I was still alive, I am not a walking dead
Yearning for a song.
Candles, crowd and gifts have had their days,
Like flowers, had faded.

Above my head the sky was blue and clear
Blooms were still warm in the sun's embrace
And the crazy bees still intent and insatiable.

But in my loneliness, I could not afford to be
uncertain.
My mind ran, caught into a spider's web.
The more so as evening and darkness closed in.
I looked at the sky
And prayed, oh Lord send me someone!

I seek no name nor fame
No miracle nor wealth,
Cannot someone come and sing for me today?
Just, I pleaded.

Before my last word fell out,
A black bird landed on my apple tree
And exploded into an spectacular trill of delightful
warbling
Lasting till sunset

I wonder sometimes if we are really alone,
Who knows, somewhere someone is following our tears
And smiles.

THE MOON WILL WAIT.

Little I know the place I came to
And the shore I landed on.
Little I know the way that leads to heaven
Or to hell!

Little I know on whose door to knock.

Some let me in and fondly invite me to sup with
them.
Others dismiss me with scorn, ignore my hunger.

My journey is unchartered, an open field of
struggle,
A bloom aspiring for the sun
Made sacrosanct by an unhindered choice.
But I know where it will end ..
On two pieces of wood tucked on the hill,
The will of my father.

Here we are together, different in aims and
destinations.
We labour.
We rise and fall, bruised, tears in our eyes.
We learn to win by the sweat and the sobs.
He succeeds who keeps the smile till sunset.

Around me, I read the space,
A world with stars at night
And sun in the day;
A world of hills and mountains
And valleys and lovely creatures.
But the Cross has never ceased to call.

A world of endless noise, brutality and greed
The world of man,
A ceaseless fight for tinsels and baubles
A battle of no end, where tears and smiles and
dreams
Continue to hide the frailty of this bleeding frame.

Very few know me.
Fewer seek to free me from the whips
As alone I dodder up the cobbled way in the midst of
spit
And sneers.

I have seen your eyes glow with immortal light
Beauty and ecstasy.
And I thrill to this transcendental dream,
accomplished.
In my heart, I bless my father
The moon will wait.

112

THE POET.

The song I sing
Does not belong to me.
I did not write it
Nor did I copy it from someone either.

It belongs to them
Who like me,
Love to fly their minds to the fantasy lands.

The poet's land,
Where imagination and experience
Joys and heartbreaks, delusions and dreams
Beauty and love, music and reality
Dance a most occult dance.

Of subtle beauty
Finer than the gauzy veils of early morning mist,
Soaked in emerging sunshine.
A shelter for songsters like me
To indulge in peace and visions.

There I abandon myself to the endless dance of my
mind.
 I shiver in auspicious and ecstatic freedom,
And thaw in the embrace of overpowering longings.

There I merge myself in those multiple formless
existences,
Which open my eyes to the end of infinity.
Is this a sweet delusion
Or dream maybe?

Or is it the ultimate reality?
I know.
For there I am happy,
Just disarmingly happy,
No language, no sound and no movement
Just an interminable existence.

So, drunk, I catch the wings of flitting songbirds
Which like fireflies swarm in the aureate air.
To those who do not know, the haunting tastes of
delusion
Soaked in honey which lasts long after the turmoils
In the mind and body have subsided.

But to those who know:
There is no delusion,
There is no reality,
Just the labour before the birth of a song.

OF MAN.

Oh wise men,
Condemn me not as evil.
For me the breeze blows
The sun rises
And the flowers bloom.

Yet my eyes are filled with tears,
Always.
No place to rest my head at night
Hungry.

Some have none
Others too much
Some are good, others are better.

I did not ask for war.
Yet war rages round the portals of my peace.
Nights are filled with smog and screeches
For morning breakfast, it is blood stained rubbles
Dust, groaning children, men and women.

For me stars shine
And this wondrous space ticks.
For me love flourishes and wisdom too,
Water runs, hills and mountains sit still,
The breeze blows and the sun shines.

I am man, of the creation a wonder!
The love of the Beloved,
Home to endless miracles.
Without me this universe would not be,
Its grandeur, its colours, its might
And its infinity meaningless.

But sadly from a fully braced giant,
Servile to the senses and a marauding mind
I made a confused moron of myself,

Disillusioned!
Disorientated, selfish and violent.

Now a delinquent and rowdy wolf,
A dare to him
Who once when the space was dark and pathless
On his transcendental spinning wheel,
He so lovingly wove the tissue of my glory!
From a bloom to a thorn!
From a pure and frolicking stream to a stinking
quagmire,
I have erred!

114

THE OLD WOMAN

If I could be the warmth
In the blue sky
I would gently rest your head
On a pillow of golden sunshine.

I would free your limbs
From the restless uncertainty of old age.

If I could be the cool in the early morning breeze
I would waft over your old body
And like balm, bring comfort to your shaky bones.

I wonder at those hands
Now knotty and wrinkled,

The water they had carried from the village well
The daily search for fire wood,
The clothes they had rubbed at the river.

I think of those scars
Left by the sickle,
The dry stomach
And the hungry mouth
Now thin and leathery,
All for others

Alone in your hut now
Singing songs of love
Affection and sacrifice,

In these last moments,
The birds
The beautiful sunshine
The blue sky,
And the hills and the mountains for friends,

You watch the tumultuous rush of the new era,
One of arrogance and hypocrisy,
Heartlessness and greed settling in.

You know your time is done
And you are not worried.

The smile continues to blossom

No heart aches.
You grew no thorns.

You only came to grow.
The fruits are for others to reap
And enjoy.

For once in this old world
You came empty handed.
There is nothing now you want to take with you,
Except God's love.

116

LET US WEAVE A DREAM

And when the gloom has passed,
A joyful serenity descends from the rowdy night
wind.

The village woodland explodes into a throbbing
festival
Of golden rays
As an endless display of flowers rises to greet
The struggling morning and my heart goes wild,
Frenzied for the freedom of the open air.

I grow wings and I fly.
Like the crazy bee, dressed in flying pollen of
sunlight,
I raced the shadows down to the valleys,
Like a kite I fly the world below to the wind.

I gather the blue sky in the palms of my hands
And like chaffs to the breeze, blow it with gentle
fire of love

From every tree
Down to the hungry valleys and up the hills I wake
the birds.
I fill the sky with fond flood of ecstatic light.
The air resounds with an ineffable choir of chirps
and warbles..

Endless joy,
This beautiful world was never intended to be a
place of sadness.
In the fields full of flowers,
Endless sunshine writes a new history in letters of
gold.

I will fill the hearts of those who are deprived of
hope,
I will light smiles on the lips of those who are
alone
Whose nights scream with nightmares of pains and
tears.

And when darkness has vanished
All eyes blaze forth the exuberance of this blessed
place,
I shall sit on my bed of simple straw,
Amongst the stars and the serene moonlight

I shall like fireflies rove, crazy for my own dreams
of light,
And love.

Perchance I shall find my dream.
Perchance back into my own dream
I shall make everybody's dream whole.

From every tree
Down to the hungry valleys and up the hills I wake
the birds
I fill the sky with fond flood of ecstatic light.
The air resounds with an ineffable choir of chirps
and warbles..
Endless joy,

This beautiful world was never intended to be a
place of sadness,
A reign of killer bullets
Or sickening virus!
Endless sunshine writes the new history in letters
of gold.

118

THE SOUNDS OF SILENCE

When the night is quiet,
Daubed in tranquil sheens of twinkling lights
And the stars sunk in misty reveries, distant and
waiting

In the the gentle slumbrous breeze, I hear his voice
Not like mine,

Not like yours, encompassing this place of living
marvels:
An infinite embrace,
The voice of silence.

It is an ocean, it roars.
It is a river, it runs.
It is a stream, it chatters.

It is a flood, it goes wild.
It is the crying cloud, it laments.
It is a mighty torrent, it thunders and heaves.

It sounds s the core of this heart
The cause and the sustainer of all life,
A serene and placid lake, sweet, profound and
inebriating,
Infinite!
Subtle like the flit of a life breath,
A light across the dark sky.

Catch it if you can?
No motion, irresistible.
The mad mind ceases to romp
And subdued, the senses sit still.

For those who can hear, it runs, it trills and it
pipes.
It plays and it chimes,
It enlivens and it inspires and it thrills.

Let me then sit still and attune myself
And drink deep from this inexhaustible fount,
Ceaselessly bubbling up creations from its wombs,
The voice of silence,
The mystery of the unvoiced transcendental sound.

DEEP INSIDE.

Now and then
At dusk, as the sun
Eases down towards the colour drenched horizon
I seek the shelter of the darkening shore
And wait.

I wait for myself.
My eyes close in peace.
I know the sounds of my steps,
A light rustling on the dry grass and the gullible
sand.

And in the silence,
On the sands of time
As soft as the fall of autumn leaves
Hovering to the ground,
I hear the sounds of my steps.

Little I know
How far away I was coming from:

Across areas of faded history maybe
When this world was new
And sages sat round holy fires,
Sang cryptic chants
That still like gentle morning breeze
Ring in my ears.

And I wonder at myself,
Who am I?
Ego or purity?
Light or darkness?

Loitering down the lanes of life
Slaves to insatiable senses,
I left myself behind.
I lost sight of my immanent light.

I was deep once.
Since then, caught like a fated fly
In the web of ego
I hover
Like a lost butterfly.

120

I was light once, now wallowing in rages of violence
And ignorance.
Still I know I am not lost.

Light is never lost, like the sun I bide my time to
rise.
I only receded,
Temporarily hidden behind the darkness of storm
clouds.

MY APPLE TREE IS IN BLOOM

One of the many joys of life is to see the world
Around us in bloom and happy.
A barren wasteland always screams with heartbreaks.

Our joys and our griefs are not mere mental
fabrications.
In them are the essences of our failures and
successes
Our tears and ceaseless battles to survive,
Our internal conflicts,
And our prayers!

We are not wood or stone, creatures of beguiling
destinies,
Dazed in the middle of a ruthless space
Or beggars in the middle of luxuries.

Every era knows its own ups
And down.
Up when we use the Creator's key to wisdom
And down when we choose to be pretentious and greedy
And wayward.
We end in turmoil.

We are blind to our own homily wisdom.
In our heart where love sits supreme,
Serene ecstasy points the way to ultimate happiness,
To peace and tranquility.

The lessons are here
Not there.
The learning is here,
Not there, where no one knows where!

They make the heavens and the hells.

There is joy in the bird's flight,
In the sunrise
And in the sunset,
In the warm morning breeze and the smiles,
In the glowing colours of the primroses
And in the drowsy ripples,
As they hungrily scamper for the shore.

122

And I say to myself,
Life deserves more respect than this.
I am not a trivial, insignificant piece of knead
flour,
Made to be abused.

Years after I brought it home
My apple tree is in bloom.
Is not this a miracle?
I almost sacrificed it at the altar of my
disappointment,
This morning though, it flouts my weakness of faith

THE FLOWERS WILL BLOOM.

The evening was drawing to a closed
And as darkness lumbered gradually in,
The sun wrapped up its exuberance of light and
colours
Ready for the final ease into the conflagrating
horizon.

Across the thinning woodland
The heads of the golden grass like drunks,
Swaying in the breeze,
And the air, drenched with the wondrous fragrance
Set my mind at peace.

I am a poet,
I live off the beauty of nature.
I take a blade of grass,
Dip it into the magic concoction of the flower power
And let it brew and turn gold, green, yellow and
purple.

I braid it with the tender filament of morning
sunshine,
And with endless thrill, like crystal dew drops,
Watch waterfalls of trickle down from rock to rock.

Life could be so beautiful.
Life could be full of entrancing wonders.
The flute that rises from the stream's sprightliness
The hum that makes the breeze blow,

The choir of the holy birds' vespers,
Add them up with love,
You get the eternal unsylabled symphony
That is the primal life force

Whether I go or stay, the flowers will continue to
blossom.

For they are the threads that go in to spin this
great place,
The smiles on the Maker's creation,
And love that pendants hung on the

124

ON THE HILL

They stand me on a hill
That oversees the village
And a town, wrapped up in virulent dust
And a clutter of dead structures.

My knees cry from the laughter of the whips,
And ruthless knocking
Heartless.
My eyes bleary wth dried blood, sweat and dust
And my body frail, cold in the heat of the morning
sun.

You do not know me.
I know you, who swing the whips
and sing songs of greed and inhumanity.

You hate me
But I love you.
What is hate,
And what is love, I know both.

He who knows, finds peace in his heart.
For he rises above wounds
and bleeding,
Above hate and love too.

There is only him, who sends me and you here,
Only him!
I know him
And you do not.

In your heart, seek him truely
And no fear shall be your enemy.

THE MOON WILL WAIT.

Little I know the place I came to
And the shore I landed on,
The way that leads to heaven
Or to hell!

Little I know on whose door to knock.
Some let me in and fondly invite me to sup with
them.
Others with scorn, ignore my hunger.

My journey is unchartered, an open field of
struggling life,
A bloom aspiring for the sun
Made sacrosanct by an unhindered choice.

Here we are together, different in aims and
destinations.
We labour.

We rise and fall, bruised, tears in our eyes.
We learn to win by the sweat and the sobs.
He succeeds who keeps the smile till sunset.

Around me, I read the space,
A world with stars at night
And sun in the day;
A world of hills and mountains
And valleys and lovely creatures.

A world of endless seas and oceans...
The world of man,
A ceaseless confrontation
A battle of no end, where tears and smiles combine
To grow the final glory, erstwhile hidden from him.

I have seen your eyes glow with immortal light
Beauty and ecstasy.
And I thrill to this transcendental dream,
The moon will wait.

126

LITTLE WE UNDERSTAND

One day perhaps
I shall again write a song
Woven in the tender threads of love.

One day from the hill stream,
I shall bring down the water of wisdom,
To cool the thirst of this feckless humanity.

Some say life is an unprovoked challenge,
For others it is a battle ground.
But life is us
And we are life.
We are the life and all it has to take and give.

We are the battlefield
The weapons, the Warriors,
And the enemy too.

The violence and the blood we shed,
The tears and the pain are all our own.
So spill not your own blood
Spare your heart the unwanted violence of hatred.

For life, like a tree, it grows,
Was not the sunshine made for it,
And the breeze and the immortal gift of love
And those beautiful sunrises and sunsets?

LET THE SUN RISE, LET THE SUN SET.

The morning dawns, drenched and miserable.
The birds are quiet.
Strong winds blow from a hostile sky
As thunder and lightening flog a rowdy army of dark
clouds.

Down below, starved from the warm summer sun,
A cemetery of sallow rose petals on the slabs,
It is miserable!
Earth sobs for a cup of the elixir sunshine.

I hate to lose hope; so quietly in my heart,
I collect sticks of resolutions and a handful of
shredded joys
And put them together.
I watch the light glowing.

New life shivers from the fire.
Life never dies, it only recedes to refurbish
itself.
A few days of unhappiness does not write a fearsome
tale.
For they only remind the soul of its own strength
and immortality.

Somewhere down pass the woodlands
Birds are still singing, sweet breeze blowing.
The shy sun is still there with basketful of shine
And nature still regales in her infinite lushness of
colours.

Some of us will certainly go.
Others will stay
For a little while longer!
Some nights will be peaceful
Others, full of terror and restlessness.

This is the way that life spins its story,
Some tears and some sunshine.
Some sun rise and some sunset to make a tissue of
continuity.
In there is the secret of the cosmic wisdom
That points to the portal of immortality.

Let the fire of faith silently burn under the ash of
despair.
We are all Phoenix, someday we will rise again.
He dies who extinguishes this fire,
He lives in peace and light
Who with faith watches over this fire of life.

THE FROZEN ROSE BUD.

And when at last
After a slow march across a starless night,
The dark drifted,
Restless
I gently moved the curtains.

My heart sank.
The frozen shroud of an ugly frost
Extended beyond the fruit trees.

Whipped by the chill of the early morning breeze,
A single yellow bud on top,
The rose bush shivered.

A frozen bud,
Was all it had to offer
To the rigour of the unconcerned winter,

A missed summer's bloom,
Frozen in time
That could neither face the future
Nor turn to the past.

Gone the sunshine
In the train of time,
Leaving behind a cold, wind-swept and deserted
station.

Like winter
Our hearts freeze now and then,

We judge,
We hurt
Little bother to think
Of the trails of pain and heartbreaks,
Left behind.
A little thoughtless pride too much, maybe!

Why oh why then do we want
To be like the frozen rose bud
In the winter of our unfriendliness,
In an unfeeling world of chilled values?

EYE OF THE STORM.

No breeze to sing in the leaves
And no sunshine to brace the woodland lanes.

Early afternoon,
The children have eased quickly back home from
school,
And the women have made short work of collecting
their water
Before the great approaching howl.
The well has sunk deeper into a threatening silence.
A storm is on its way.

Old men gaze with fear and uneasiness at the sky
And shake their heads.
It is red, ominous and full of fears.

The animals low restlessly in the sheds
As the village tucked itself behind closed doors and
windows
And wait.

A bottle of rum in his hand,
An unshaven man growled angrily at the sky
As he dangled between two blades of rising wind,
A storm!

He has nothing to lose,
No home, no family, no reason to bleed
No cross to carry,
Except for that eternal bottle of rum
Under his arms.

He swears at the villagers who sneers
He owes nothing to any one, he yells at them
Neither to God nor to man, his life is his

I wonder sometimes if, in this world of hate,
bullets and greed,
And virus, he is not right
Still escapism is not the wisdom I seek.

There was no difference between him and the bottle.
One is always half full
And the other half empty

Wind or calm
War or peace, the bottle had never stopped emptying.

And filling up
Who cares if it was a storm, he screeched at the
closing storm
Or a sunny day!
Or a baby was born

Wind, rain, rum
Storm, blood shed and babies have all always been
here
For the having, any way!

132

THE WONDER OF IT ALL.

I wander down the village slope towards the river
down below.
There I grew up
And learnt to sneak into the exuberance of nature's
secrets.
There like disdainful trolls, several boulders
stood,
In the water, on the banks and behind the bushes.

I was never able to reach the top of those huge
lumps of rocks
And sneers and pinches did not help either
Now grown up, the boulders seem to have shrunk.
And it takes me a simple hitch to get on top.

But all the friends have gone
The echoes of shrill screeches
And the youthful madness have long quietened.
Some of the friends have moved, some have passed
away,
The rest have forgotten about the river and the
boulders.

From its old rapid and bouncy verve,
The river has shrunk into a sickly flow of mire and
mud
Throttled with weeds, dead leaves, except when it
rains
And the fierce floods tumble down from the hills.

The boulders have sunk into the ground.
Like all things one day they will not be there
either.
It has never bothered me that things come and go.

This is the way life goes.

Some flowers are new, some have waned , on the way
out,
New birds and new songs
New monkeys and new chatters,
There is nothing any one can do about it.

Even the displays on the hills' are not the same:
The green has turned into a brilliant gold and
yellow,
The wild hibiscus was pink the week before, now
purple.
Life is in a constant and continuous flux.

So are we!
The beauty and wisdom of it all lie in its eternal
self refurbishing,
A smooth unenforced flow
A serene and an enchanting processing
Very deep, sustained and tense.

TO BE OR NOT TO BE.

As a drowsy breeze waltzed in the dust
And darkness hailed the parting of an exhausted day,
The temple bells echoed their last vespers,
And silence eased in on the village.

It had been a hot day all day,
One of those days that turned the village woodland
rocks
Into hot plates
And made the roadside clumps of reeds droop.
I sought the coolness of a chestnut tree on the
shore

And watched the stars studding the dark sky.
As the sea seethed in the gentle moonlight.
How strange is this stupendous and infinite place!
How audaciously exuberant the peace!

Like fronds in the early morning breeze,
My mind shivered at its wonders,
A soft shawl of serenity hovered down from the
twinkling infinity.

Ecstatic!
My eyes flowed!
It was Him, so lovingly, so shyly
Hiding behind, so silently spinning those tissues of
rapturous hues
Into forms and shapes!

It took the sky and the stars
It took the hills and the mountains
It took me , you and everything.

Sun shines,
Rains fall and tender buds of staggering snow
showers,
Gently berthed by the hum of an unhampered breeze,
Seen and unseen!

I heard sounds of harp
And running water,
Rings of church bells and choir of chirping birds,
Conches and harmless thunder roars,
Waves after waves!

That wrote my own destiny in this breathtaking
creation!
For He who made the stars and the moonlight
The daylight and the thriving life, made me as well.
Time may stop but his spinning continues.

WHEN YOU   SEE THE SUN TOMORROW

When the sun rises
And this place brims with the magic of aureate sun
beams
Uninhibited, let me drag this diddering frame out of
bed,
Steal downstairs,
No socks, no shoes, like a child
To abandon myself to the abundance of the sun filled
delights!

Do not stop me, I will forget my pain.
I will forget my heartbreaks and fears.

I will not forget that I am on the last beads of
life!
For as much as we say there is only despair here,
So much more are there unseen joys.

Let me sit by the dark bushes of wild hibiscus,
Of purple and pink blooms
White and blended turquoise,
Old friends of mine that are always welcoming.
Do not be dismayed by your mortality,
It is a transcendental blessing.

Oh Lord the smell of gun smog is strong in the air!
The raucous thuds of cannons outside my windows
And the rattling of guns have shaken the stars all
night.
The village fields bloom with unwanted tears and
bullets.

I still care when the birds sing
When in the early afternoon the black bird yodels,
I still care when the tiny redbreast robin exhibits
his ecstasy,
frenzy at the sight of a wriggly grub.

Let me then pull the curtain
And flush the room with showers of daylight,
For who knows what will the poor night bring?
Let me pray that the day never ends
And the night never comes.

I must learn to accept both the gentleness
Of the cool breeze
And the harshness of the bad wind.

How weird is this life!
When the guns are quiet, peace is elusive,
And when peace is here, I miss the guns's laughters.

Man must play,
With toys
Or guns!
Let me out in the sunshine,
And when the night sets in and gentle slumber
overtakes my eyes
I shall gently claim the infinity that is mine.

LEAN ON HIM A LITTLE.

Let joy possess you.
When it rains and you are drenched
Say it is a blessing.

When you trust your near and dear
And they let you down
And your eyes are full of tears, your heart of pain
Bless them, pray for them!

When strangers surround you with arms of love
And bright smiles
And you feel enlivened and robust,
Praise Him who acts so subtly.

We till the mind as we till the land.
We take care to grow flowers only.

Some thorns are bound to appear,
Sometimes more thorns than blooms.

Stand still and whimper, and you are possessed
By dust and tears.
You give your mind a further chance to tread you
down.
The load and the way are yours, accept them!

From somewhere beyond this sun and the moon,
This stupendous facade and this crowded space
Someone wants you to lean on Him!

Silently He is renewing your strength
Carrying your load,
Walking besides you, how could he ever leave you?

138

A   CHILD   AT   PLAY.

Something in the gold of the morning sunshine
Told me that there will be magic in the air
And I wandered towards the village well,
A transparent and blue sky
Lending a friendly welcome.

Near the well, thoroughly absorbed, a little girl
was playing
A game of lithe movements, skipping and giggling
Now and then adding a shrill peal of laughter,
Unaware of the big world around her.

Like dry leaves in the breeze
Ideas floated into my mind, uncontrollable
Silently spinning threads of poetry,
No sound, no word
Just a random flow.

Play on child
Play on before this world catches up with you!
Stay free, guard yourself from being the hunted one!

In that childlike innocence and exuberance,
Be it in the fields of life,
In a cultured garden
Or by the busy roadside of life, play on!

Till nightfall,
This frail frame is gently berthed in the magic
Of nightly slumber,
Till across the fields of dreams
Your feet have sauntered like gentle snowflakes.
Your life is a dream,
Let no fear wake you up!

Oh beautiful sleep of a child!
Oh gentle, carefree sleep of a child,
To nothing comparable!

Look not over your shoulders
Where life rages
And opiating flowers of lies, pains, greed and
hatred
bloom wild.

A gentle flower,
Today by loving arms, protected.
Who knows who can look into the seeds of time
And say what tomorrow brings.
Love them while you may.

Today they will dry your tears
Tomorrow perchance you will nurse their broken
hearts!
Let no storm possess your heart
Nor hate steal those beautiful colours of your
cheeks,
Let your eyes for ever remain gentle.

Your innocence is your protection
And your protection is your dream,
Only that you do not know it is a dream,
That one day, it will burst and fill your eyes with
agonizing tears

One day you will wake up
And find your games and the rules have changed,
Ruthlessly carried down the tunnel of the past,
Irretrievable!
You will wonder perhaps
And ask yourself why has everything become so
callous:

Your heart will have hardened,
Your world as slippery as an eel
Your hands as lined and dry as mine.
You will then doubt your mirror,
And call it a liar!
Sadly this is the only time when a lie is the truth.

Stay a child, for ever.
Play on while the sunshine of innocence lasts,
While the butterflies are still in love with you.
Play on while the gentle voices of your mum and dad

Still sound sweet to your ears!
And your heart is tender!

140

COME WITH ME.

Come with me
I will take you
To where poetry like fire flies
Lark in the smooth exuberance of the tender night.

Where the serene village lake gleams
In pageantry of morning sunshine,
Where in wild freedom flowers bloom
And the lone wood pigeon
Explodes each morning in endless ditties of love
songs.

There freedom is free
And God is God,
Not a weapon
Bullet or bomb on warpath,

Or a selfish fabrication
Set in the arena of sultry hatred
To battle it out against himself.

I will take you
Where the machinery of this life
Is run with faith and devotion.

Come with me
To the warm and lush belts of sunshine,
Abandon yourself to the warm pour of the summer rain
Soak soak soak!

Where no brutal wind howls
Or like hungry wolves
Fear stands on the other side of the door.

There life beams of light sublime
And cascades tumble from on high
Scattering sprays of ceaseless joy and hope.

There you will live on the human level,
Still not found by many.
To know that you are human
Is to know that you are shaking the shackles of
ignorance,
A God in the making.

Come with me
To where no harsh words
Shall cause your heart to ache.
I will fill your uncertain sky
With abundance of ineffable peace.

Together we shall brave the night
And wait for the sun to rise.
He who made the sun

Did not make it for a day.

For those who wants it dearly
The sun will always rise.

142

WHO WAS IT WHO MADE IT ALL?

The temple bells have rung
Sweet music of silence invades the air
As darkness hails the parting of an exhausted sun.

It has been hot all day,
One of those days that turn the village woodland
rocks
Into hot plates
And made the roadside reeds droop.

Like my flock of goats, I had sought the shade
And shared with them the rare and stray blessing of
a cool breeze,
And blew on my reed pipe.

Now at quiet, sitting in front of my shed
I look at the stars
And wonder at whoever made them.

He who made them made me too, surely
And my goats and my dog and the wondrous valley
Down below the slope, pass the old cemetery!

I love to feel that I am not alone,
He is somewhere near who made it all.
He hides in the valley behind the blooms.

He paints the sun rise
And the sunset.
I have not seen the sea, but they say he is there
too
And in the tender little brook that babbles all day
and night.

Is not this lovely?
Maybe I ought to look for him.
He must be a wonderful guy to give us so many a
beautiful thing.
And free too!

HAVE YOU SEEN HIM?

Night and day
Your names continue to echo In my heart
And Your image fill my mind's eye.
I seek Thee far and wide,
everywhere,
And yet I see thee not,

Still from the serene warmth of the valley's sunlit
shadows
The breeze brings a waning strain of your flute.

Tears in my eyes
Sobs choking my heart I loiter in vain,

Near the river
Near the pond
Down the village slope
No one has seen you.

The villagers laugh at my naivety
And ask if I have ever seen the wind,
Or the willow stop crying.

I watch the flowers' ecstatic sways, like possessed
Fanning colours and fragrance.
They too dance to the tunes of your flute,
Naughty! naughty! They say you are.

The will- o- the wisp of the dusky evening sun
The shimmers in the fleeting runs of the ripples on
the pond,
That teasing the heart is your favourite pastime.

The enchanting sounds of your flute
And your fleeting fragrance
Caught in the starry spinning of the crazy nights
Are dear memories of rare encounters.

Oh crazy me!
I say to myself
Why do I search for the unsearchable?

If I cannot catch the breeze
Nor the mystic fragrance of the queen of the night
If I cannot stop the ripples from dying on the
sunset shores
Nor catch the dance of fleeting shadows on the
hills,

How then can I catch the uncatchable,
He who has no frame nor form?

It is my love that gives him form.
The way is not out there
But in here, in my heart
where only I
And him can tread.

This is why the flowers
And the breeze are silent
The villagers and the hills are stunned
For He is your own special and personal experience.

TEARS OF THE EARTH.

When I see flowers
I thrill to the beauty of God.
When I find the sun has risen
I say to myself God has created another day.

Another marvel for me,
And for you
So that after a night's rest
We can by true living embark on our journey back to
him.

Life is action
And action is life,
Both important parts of faith
And prayer.

Prayer without action is lip service to the Creator,
It makes beggars of us.
He has given me light to see,

Freedom to choose
And to rise above the mundane,
Mind to understand the wide screen play around us
And to fit it to his infinity.
For in us are both the finite and the infinity.

That which comes must one day go,
Man makes a sordid tragedy of it.
The wise,
The Avatars and the prophets,
The poor and the rich,
No one comes to stay.

They grow old too and finally depart,
For this world is itself here at the will of the
Creator.
So the wise sees death as another way to
immortality,
A celebration of the splendor of the Soul.

Cry not
This earth has seen more pain than you can imagine.
No one has shed more tears than her,

Watching her children
One after another hopelessly carried by the current
of time.

Her heart is not hard
But tender.
Her tears only go to enrich and fortify herself
That makes it a more welcoming haven for her future
children.

146

LET THE LIGHT ON

Slowly from behind the mountains
The sun rises
Spreading an inefable splendour of colours below.

I thrill to the touch of the subtle rays
As they gently pass me by
Carried on the wings of a vagrant breeze.

And I stop
And listen.
There is a sound there,
There is a voice, light, deep and profound,
A chant, unsylabled that says, let the light on!

A voice in the leaves and in the breeze,
In the cascade below the hills
Calling from the cracks of mountain rocks!

A voice in the air as the birds dive across the blue
sky
A voice in the bush as flowers bloom.
A voice in the air as the frolicsome bee hungrily
thirsts
For honey.

A song in the infinite and open firmament
As the maker plays on his flute
And the night sky explodes in an exuberance of
smiling lights.

I look into my heart to find my own little song of
light,
I cry
My heart whimpers and sobs
And with all my God given might

In the waking woodland I raise my voice to all the
hearts.
Let the light on
For ever
And for ever.

THE ROADSIDE FLOWER.

I stand by the roadside,
A flower, tender but wild,
Child of parents unknown.

Blown by the breeze and the winds
To where I am abused by the eternal ravages of
dusts,
Harsh weather
And my beauty ignored.

Nights pass
And days too, I sob quietly in my loneliness.
The sunshine flutters pass me in the morning
But the warmth hardly ever reaches my heart
Confined under by a shroud of dust.

When the weather is calm
I watch those beautiful crocuses
And blue bells further down the slope
Where the trees are high
And the shade is warm.

I watch laughing children picking them
Do they ever think that I am a flower also
And beautiful, good to be offered to a loved one?

The pain in my heart redoubles,
I cry
And I say to myself
I am here through no fault of mine,.
 Caught into the web of a dusty life

No one has ever tried to see how beautifulI I am!
I only know of unwarranted disdain.
No one has ever looked into my heart
To see my real beauty and purity.

No one has tried to lift this veil of dust from my
face,
And made a bride of me!
My misfortune is that I bloomed in the wrong place,
Not in a park nor in a garden.

Whoever wrote my destiny,
Did me injustice.
But remember
Gold and diamonds are born in the dust too,
Only love reveals their brilliance and glow.

THE SONG OF THE MYSTIC SONGBIRD

It sings.
Ceaselessly.
Night and day
Day and night,
A continuous and uplifting saga.

Now of a conch sound
Then church bell
And trickling water.
Now a rolling thud of thunder
A roar of the ocean.
And a prayerful chirp of homing birds.

But stop, it does not.
It changes.
It furls
And it sprays like a fancy cascade.
Still I can hardly tell
From where it comes.

Not from the wood.
Not from the bush of bougainvilleas
That decks the village well
Where children play
And women chatter.

Neither the hills nor the mountains
Have known song
So honeyed
And inebriating.
Astounded
They sit still.

Sweeter than those strummings in the trees
Ditties of the breeze in the morning
As it strolls from far and wide,
An enlivening mystery.

It stirs.
It soars.
It creates.
As like the sprays of a waterfall,
Reality and fantasy tumbling out.

150

Like the string

That passes through the hearts of the flowers
Holding the garland,
It holds the past and the present
The future too.

All on a sudden time seems to be only
A ridiculous piece of unclocked chase,
An unbroken horse.

They say time does not stop.
But it does
When I am drowned in that song,
That mellow and transcendental strain
Which thrills
And I say to myself

Without it, the sky would not be so blue,
The air so light and aureate
The flowers so exciting.

As I sit quiet
And drink from it.

And in the serenity
Hills and mountains
Blossom.

Breeze blows
And rivers run
And endless garlands of creation rise and fall
Still the mystic song pipes on.

DO NOT BE FOOLED BY TIME.

As alone I sat on the shore playing my flute
The old man stopped,
Grinned but said nothing.
Eyes moist.

The evening sun had dimmed,
And a cool breeze, arduously
driving the ripples up to the line of grass,
Had called a rest.

I could not see the breeze,
But I have learned to see when it is tired
and breathless.

It reminded me of myself,
Old now and alone.
It is not a tragedy, it is just the old inevitable
way,
The one old road through vistas of waterfalls
And greenery,
Pass which you never come back.

Same joys maybe
Same love for flowers and green grass
Same old delights in the birds' yodels
And flaunt of the clouds
As they return home in the gathering gloom.

Life has always had two ends.
One when it began
And the other when it ends,
The rest is forgetfulness.

The breeze says I still love you.
And the children are still there to pamper you,
The sunset says I will come again.
Wait for me to rise after dark.

In the meantime keep a tryst with the stars.
We do not shed tears, see!
These are drops of dews,
Love from above.

It is beautiful to live,
But it has never been a tragedy to leave.
Life has never ended since once it began,
We only stop walking for a while.
We are in the other side of the mirror
We come back again to greet the same sun.

152

I SMELL A STORM

No breeze to sing in the leaves
And no sunshine to brace the woodland lanes.

Early afternoon,
The children had eased quickly back home from school
And the women had made short work of collecting
their water.
Before the great howl on the way,
The well had sunk deeper into a deserted
And threatening silence

Old men gazed with fear and uneasiness at the sky
And shook their heads.
It was red, ominous and full of fears.

The animals lowed restlessly in the sheds
As the village tucked itself behind closed doors and
windows
And waited.

A bottle of rum under his arm,
An unshaven man growled angrily at the sky,
As he dangled between two blades of rising wind,
A storm!

He had nothing to lose,
He never had anything.
He was born with empty hands,
Except for the bottle rum, they were still empty.

There was no difference between the bottle
And him.
One is always half empty
And the other half full.

Wind or calm
War or peace, the bottle had never stopped emptying.
Who cares if it was a storm, he screeched at the
closing storm
Or a sunny day?
Or a baby was born?

Wind, rain, rum
Storm, blood shed and babies, have all always been
here
For the having, any way!

SEEK ME, NOT MY GIFTS

Beauty has no definition nor form
What is fair to you is foul to me
And what is fair to me is foul to you.

I love the warm rain pouring down from the running
clouds
And I surrender to the magic of its subtle patters.
Inebriated, wet and warm, life thrills in me
And slowly blazes to a bonfire.

I am a poet,
Older than the crazy run of time,
And I fantasize in creating.

At a sweep of my thoughts,
Worlds and civilizations rise and fall,
Stars stud the dark sky
Planets bounce in empty space,
Suns rise and Suns set.

Into my concoction, I throw in grains of wisdom and
colours
Smiles and tears, anger and peacefulness
Love and violence.
I am no saint, I am human.
My mind dangles between the beginning and the end.

A bit of sunset and a bit of sunshine,
A splash of the babbling brook,

Some scented flowers of the dew drenched valleys,
Add glows of tender star lights, and I stir.
Space, universes, world emerge, sprout and spread.

Know it whoever will.
Love it whoever will.
I am the beginning and I am the end.
I am love, I am wisdom and I am ecstasy!

154

I am good and I am evil.
The glory of all glories, I am sunshine and I am
darkness.
Choose my sunny side
And inherit endless heritages of happiness
From my dark side, only tears follow.

Pull your curtains of ignorance
And stars of hope and light
Infinity is a breath away.

Catch the marvel of my mystery,
I dance
Fanning planets and starlight in the darksome space
An ecstatic dance of ceaseless creation!

Listen to my roar in the turbulent ocean
My laughter in the rowdy gales
And the sounds of my transcendental flute.

Watch my glory in the sunset

My joy in sun rise.
And in your heart,
Seek my peace in the untroubled ocean of serenity.

I never cease to give.
Seek me, the eternal giver and find in me eternal
repose
But he who is contented with my gifts seldom find
peace,
And ends in heartbreaks.

For my gifts are ephemeral.
I alone am eternal, limitless.
Seek me, child, not my gifts,
And be for ever happy!

WHO AM I?

I am light,
I am darkness.

I am the way and I am the glory.

In wisdom
Like the radiant sun
I wax in light.

In darkness, like the pale moon
I wane,
And this fragile frame suffers
Victim to consumming distresses.

Like the wonton waterfall tumbling from on high
Spilling showers of gleaming sunshine
I am happiness.

In patience, I am a fortress
Of rock and stone,
Fearless
Treading the path of self-realisation.

And in ignorance, I am a shack of straw
My mind a tinderbox,
Slave to the marauding senses
Silently consuming myself.

At the dawn of wisdom,
In the heart of the transcendental light,
I see myself as the glory of the One
Who made me.

No light, no darkness
No wisdom nor happiness, my fringes
I see myself as Him
And Him as me,
The ultimate reality of consciousness.

156

WAKE ME UP.

Let me be.
Just be,

Nothing more.

There is war in time,
Trapped into a funnel
Where life clogs,
And stinks of warring smog.

Some like the smell of spilled blood,
And the shrill laughter of flying bullets;

Others,
Like me more gentle,
In the bower of life seek a tender shade
Where sweet smell of incense hovers in the air
And love blossoms.

This world has changed, love:
A seething turmoil now
A restless place
Caught into the sticky embrace of a breathless
configuration.

Blessed is he then, who in this insane change, could
snatch
A moment of peace to look into himselfo
And enjoys the infinity that was always his,
Serenity in peace
And peace in uncertainty.

I raise my eyes
And find the withered blooms coming to life,
For they never died
And I rejoice.

Colours blaze trails of hope,
And divine fragrances constantly spinning tissues of
new life.
Your hatred
And your bullets lie buried in the filth of selfish
dreams.

There is joy,
New gentle joy.
Crestfallen,
War squirms defeated.
Life has vindicated itself.

You can shatter the stars
And shake the moon.
You can dry the ocean
And obliterate the sun,
But I still am
The eternal am!

Still the same old vessel of love
Which neither you nor I can destroy
I am and know I am.
And you are
And know not that you are.

158

THIS LIFE IS FOR REAL   Double.

Who says
That this life
Is a fabricated dream,
A harrowing deception,
That spawns unjustifiable suffering?

Treat not the Lord, love
As sadistic,
Even insensible.
Not a sparrow falls from the tree
That does not break his heart.

In his consciousness, this cosmic extravaganza
Is even less than the size of a mustard seed,
Trusted to man.
He did not house man into a fateless bubble
Rolling across the uncertain space for selfish glee.

Think of the innumerable dangers,
This earth encounters;
Comets, black holes, meteors
Are but a paltry few.

Yet by love,
The sun continues to rise
And set,
Rain to fall
And from barren soil life to rise.
Birds dare the storms at the top of precarious
bushes

And man learn to prosper by his holy sweat.
All
With wondrous,
Effortless and meticulous ease.
Suffering sometimes makes fools of us,
And turns us into ignorant judges.

We build fortresses in our minds
And set our freedom prisoner,
And make a weapon of our dreams.

Seek not to ignore this place,
Where buds beget flowers
Bees honey
And the soul learns to excel
The impermanence of this fragile displays.
Guided by the ancient wisdom,
Seek not to possess it, as elusive as fireflies it
is.

This is a renewable reality,
A cosmic idea in perpetual reconditioning
Always a perfect fit, in all circumstances
Every time,
Every season.

After feeding this fragile frame to the cosmic flame
Like from the bud we rise, a full fledge flower.

160

THE NIGHT VIGIL.

Around me the village is quiet.
And the wait gets more tedious and tearful.
Those sounds of morning footsteps may never come
again.
Life has become a scare!
A nightmare,
Maybe a retribution!

And death?
A rowdy and gorging predator!
An insatiable dark monster!

Am I going to wake up the next day?
Like the fabled falls of ripe fruits,
Humanity disintegrates, slowly.
Faith cries as dusts collect in the holy places,
Uncertainty and fear in our hearts.

Whoever dares, continues to live,
With death as bedfellow,
Keeps the light of night vigil on
A febrile hope in his heart.

Still there have been beautiful days before,
Full of aureate sunshine.
The day has never ceased to break
Nor the beauty of the sun to embellish
the wonders of this place.

Caught in darkness many a time
Man's head had bent before,
In hopelessness.

But from the ash of dismay, like the Phoenix
had never failed to rise again,
Refurbished and fortified,
new vigour and new determination.

It is easy to die
Or to end a life.
But It takes grit and mettle to live,
And mount new visions,
Far more strength and endurance to sustain the
tension
On the bow of life.
Meet then the test with a smile!

THE RIGHT WAY IS ALWAYS RIGHT.

Not many rivers flow to merge with the sea!
Not all flowers bloom to reach the altar of God.

Whipped by winds and storms
Seared by the noonday heat, they wilt
Waiting for the coolness to be kinder
and the tomorrow more enlivening.

For many tomorrow is a chimera
A figment, a mere ideation, a day after a long
sleep,
An illusion in the mind of man,
It never comes.

Before the coming of the coolness,
The river dries,
The flowers wane.

One by one,
Like dewdrops, the petals fall
Back into the arms of the loving mother,

That gave them birth.
Like the rivers and the bees, we loiter down the
lanes of life
In search of happiness and greatness.

Unhappy man can only chant of unhappiness
World of living illusions
Can only ultimately engender illusions
And tears.
Blessed is he who finds permanent happiness in this
world.

162

Life is like grains of sands,
It is constantly slipping through the fingers.
Those are great Souls who have mastered
The laws of holding the grains from losing.
They are the masters of life and illusions.

One day perchance when we learn to stop
Counting the pages of our own puny successes,
And broaden our visions of what this world is really
about
The secret will be revealed to us of the immortal
reality.

We will see
That our mind and heart have been hijacked
By the ignorance of our marauding senses,
That unknown to us,
We have been going the wrong way all along.

The truth and the way are what those wise men left
behind
to guide us,
But which we turned our backs on for a quick brew of
success.
The rest is continuous confusion
And suffering.

THE OLD FISHERMAN.

Who says
That the sea has no emotion?

The old fisherman laughs,
For he knows better.
His life is a tissue
Tumultuously woven with threads of ripples and
billows,
Rise and fall
Fall and rise.

At day break
When the first ray of the sun glimmers
Through screens of warm vagrant mist,
He stands on the shore,
Scanning the horizon once visible,
calm
And friendly,
A safe invitation.

Now old,
Limbs unreliable,
Eyes sunken, glazed like the waning moon
Face sallow and scrawny,
And scarred by the relentless rays of the midday
sun,
He watched the sea,

Not the same,
Not his sea.
Now restless, threatening
Over-flooding, chafing
Unfriendly
Like an old friend turned hostile;

That had in one night of screeching anger
Shattered his boat,
A sad relic
Lying back up under the almond tree
Shelter for stray cats.

The sea has no religion
No colour
No hate nor love.
He knew it.
But he still wonders where has all that calmness
gone

164

THE CRY Of THE WOUNDED BIRD

There was a rustle in the leaves in the back garden

As a black bird slid out in sight, dragging a broken
wing,
In pain, helpless and panting.

For a moment, he was quiet.
In my heart I could almost hear his groans and
prayers,
As tears gathered into my own eyes.

Oh God, be kind to me!
Listen to the prayer of this helpless child.
The babies are waiting.
This earth is not my home.

I live higher up.
Now in the hills aglow with blooms,
Then where beautiful cascades fall
And sing your love.

My home is in the air
Where the clouds are light and playfull
And the sky is blue.

At night
I watch the stars decked with tinsels of gold,
And the moon light my home and lulls me to sleep.

Oh God the bird in me yearns to fly
And vie with the fleeting exuberance of the morning
sunshine
And drink deep from the azure sky

The bird in me wants to sing,
For my heart bubbles with songs of the air and the breeze
How shall I tell it to remain quiet?

For me time is standing still now.
My songs cry in my heart,
And my freedom curtailed.

In the morning the temple bells call.
I shed tears.
My heart breaks
As the stray arrows of sunshine tickle me
And I die to rear up.

Oh God have mercy!
Let me pour my love for you in my songs,
Let my freedom be the garland
That every morning I bring to you,
Or let me die heart broken, for ever grounded.

166

A TRYST WITH THE HEART.

There are in this lovely universe
Many a subtle thing that the mind cannot reckon with
And dubs them as vague, fictitious or lotus eaters'
dreams,
And even evil.

So I left the mind behind,
The arguments and the clamours too.
My heart was crying to be alone.

As the dark deepened,
A streak of light lingered in the remote sky.
The stars were shyly waiting behind veils of
hurrying mist
And a fresh breeze was blowing gently from the sea.

Stop, my heart warned.
Listen!
There is wisdom in this serenity
And music in the air.
Dressed into an array of living aureate shimmers,
The moon is so bewitching?

But I could hear nothing
And saw less.
I was as closed as a tight box.

Said my heart
I can hear the hills' breaths, keen, restless, but
happy.
I wonder why like fireflies does the breeze rove in
thirsty wander?
Why is this place locked into a frenzy of breathless
waiting.

I can guess who is coming,
I can feel his steps,
Light like the fleeting morning sunshine.

Ecstatic,
The woodlands, the sea, the birds scream in frenzied
silence,

They cry for the sight of him
Whose flute breathes life and power
Joys and love.
In that sweet turmoil they know he is near.

Like my heart
Why could I not express him then?
Why like this endless panoply of things
I could not explode in the same ineffable wanton
Of adoration too?
This I asked my heart.

Like them you have them all,
But you chose to forget.
You chose the transient.
Sit quiet like the hills
Rise gently from your bud inside!

This place was once yours too,
You lost it in trying to possess it.
Shake your false pride and your greed
Surrender your restlessness and your fake knowledge.
Come naked forth.
And shine in your prestine purity.

You will then know that the soundless has sounds,
Unsyllabled and transcendental,
That like the rays of the sun,
Wisdom and knowledge
Beauty and peace
Love, bloom from the same fount.

168

IN SEARCH OF THE CREATOR.

By whatever name you call your God
He is my God also,

Whatever form you think of Him
Form or formless
He is my God also.

There is only one of Him,
Some look for him in holy and structured places
Others sit under a tree with closed eyes.
Still others wait praying in their hearts,
There is no place in which he is not.

All names are his
And all forms.
He answers to all forms
And all names.
He is neither mine nor yours.

He is wise who unrestricted in heart and mind
Makes a holy place of his heart,
Who sees this world and star studded sky as his home
And all creatures great and small
As his children.

We would not go wrong then
For we would know where to find him,
Not far from ourselves,
In our hearts.

A LITTLE FAITH GOES A LONG WAY.

Whoever seeks the way,
Trusts himself
Faith in his heart, will find it.

Still some loiter
And lose the way.
For those who live by the senses
Will loiter with the senses,
They only last with this frail frame.

To him who has faith, grace blazes the way
For faith is the way, the strength and the goal.
Faith is the guiding star.

Still the way needs to be faced,
To be contended with to earn grace.
Many a thing has to be sorted.
Like us, Saints and Avatars came by the grace
The hard way too.

When once God needed us
Opiated by the senses, we turned our back on him.
The world and the senses our gods.

We flogged him.
We crucified him.
We slandered and chased him.
We even stoned and banished him to heartless
forests.

He gave us a choice
And few chose the right way.
Not that he is now taking revenge.
God is love
Even the sinner finds peace at his feet, say the
wise men.

He is near,
He is always near to give us a helpful nudge.
He is aware of our weakness,
That we are inclined to err.

His heart is tender and his love immeasurable.
His mind is always engaged in getting us,
The Spirit in us, back to him.

NO END OFJOY

That night my heart almost stopped with wonder
Like thousands of fireflies caught in a race
Of explosive excitement,
Rising, rising towards the street lights;
There was poetry in the air.

The breeze was warm
And tender.
The stars were quiet and remote
Setting my mind on fire.

She was back, dressed in gold

Not far,
Not near, a big round face.
She was here spelling a charm only home to her.

In the quiet of the night
She tickled the flowers
And spates of perfume fanned through the drunken
air.

I know her,
She was going to stay till the first light of dawn
When the hills and mountains hailed the glow of the
rising sun.
The sea rose from its tumultuous dreams
And the restless bird broke the shackles of his
narrow straw cell
In wild ditties of ecstatic warbling.

I watched her
As in a wide sweep of tender moonbeams
she flings her dress around
Sending displays of golden tinsels in the air
Leaving the stage to the mighty sun.

172

HOPE WILL SURVIVE.

That morning
The sun rose early
And drove the rowdy spates of cold shadows
That like tattered shrouds
Haunted the lonely village wood.

From the pages of the new born day
I read hope.

Strange how the days run.
I am old now
The sky is not the same
And the sun rays hurt.

Those lovely hills
And mountains,
Once treasure troves of endless inspirations,
Have lost their exuberance.
Patches of ugly dryness hurt my heart.

Some of us rise with the threats of thunder clouds
And lightening too.
Others are welcome with lush sunshine
And smiles
And hope blossoms.

Still others,
After a searing night of warring despair
Wake up with threats of bloodshed
And songs of flying bullets.

Shrivelled in buds
Peace writhes in pain.
This is the language of the new world.

This the time
When tender flowers bear thorns,
And love spawns heartless hatred,

Outcome of educated trash
And ignorance,
When behind screens of vague and suspicious
knowledge,
wisdom cries alone

Once we grew flowers.
Once we grew love.
Now morphed by spiritual liars
They wane in confused hearts.

This is not your world
Nor mine.
It is his who made it.

Despite songs of bullets
And thunders of empty haranguing
Cows will continue to bear milk,
Lambs will be born

Humanity is here to stay.
The sun will continue to rise
And the moon to call the night in.

As long as light of faith burns in this frail frame
Hope will survive
For one candle is enough to light a thousand more.

174

WHEN NIGHT SPEAKS.

When the wind has finally rested,
Night blooms slowly like from a bud,
Opening its petals of mellow darkness,
A subtle and rolling display of dark haze
studded with serene stars.

The village slumbers.
My eyes rejoice in their freedom as for a while
alive and thrilled,
I could watch the night come to roost;

Like a frail pigeon
I grow wings and gently fly to many a fantasy land,
Of dreams and make -believes.

For not all nights are stalked by nightmares
And street terrors.
Not all nights rattle with murderous machine guns
And wandering bullets.

There are still in this wonderful artifact of God
Many a thing of surpassing beauty.
Some may have lost faith but faith is not dead yet.

So I leave my mind to wonder,
To wonder amongst the multifarious treasures
Of nightly thrills;
Tender breeze, changes of colours in the sky
And hosts of fireflies and stars.

You sleep and you do not see them.
You do not hear them,
The ceaseless buzzing of the cicadas
The howls of a stray dog,

The sounds of the breeze in the trees.
You do not see behind a closed door,
The halo of light of a single oil lamp wavering.

And when the night is clear, you do not see
Boats of star lights sailing across the sky,
Or a spooky bat flying, hungry.

Then the rarest sight of all, the spirit of the
night,
Running flashes of light snaking crazily
in the remote and emblazoned emptiness above.

Like thousand little wicks of light
They wander in the mellow cloudless sky.
Like thousands little bells, they tinkle.

Like the chants of silence, the eternal hum
Throwing up waves after waves of creation,
From an inexhaustible fount.

They reach close to your heart and hug you
And you ask yourself why your eyes are wet.
These are real,
Not imagined dreams,
Not to be had in sleep!

When you are in the opiating embrace of sleep
That takes you to the heart of the dream worlds.
You change reality for fantasy,
It is not the same when you wake up!

Humanity
Animals
Nature sleep, how innocent,
How beautiful, how sweet!
But how fake!

Wise men do not sleep.
Eyes closed, they sit up and watch within themselves
The finest concoction of wisdom brewing.

176

A NIGHT VISIT

Sometimes at nightfall
I hear your steps, quiet, light
And childlike
And your breathing, stealthy
Like a naughty child sneaking up the stairs.

I would run
To catch a sight of you.
You are very mischievous, every body knows that
I know it too.

The least noise I make

You would start your eternal pranks
And it would take me a long long time again before I
find you
Although you would be no further from me
Than from my own self.

That night the door banged close
And you were gone, heartbroken I sat on the stairs,
Cursing myself for being naive and negligent
And noisy.

In the morning I found the kitchen floor smeared
with traces of butter and I said to myself,
No one would ever know how blessed I was.

MY KINGDOM

In a dream I was a king.
No kingdom
No queen and no pageantry,
No ministers and no horses,
I was a king.

I surveyed my kingdom.
Wisdom was my first minister
Love and peace, .beauty and honesty, my subjects.
And plenty and happiness my closest friends.

Surrounded with barbed wires, under tight
surveillance,
I gave my prisoners no reprieve.

All powerful and irresistible, vindictive and
surreptitious ,
They are always ready to subvert.

My prisoners,
Anger, dishonesty, lies, violence and greed were
kept
Under lock and key.
Thus the story went, my kingdom was affluent.

178

SEEK ME NOT MY GIFTS.

Beauty has no definition nor form
What is fair to you is foul to me
And what is foul to you is fair to me

I love the warm rain pouring down from the running
clouds
And I surrender to the magic of its subtle patters.
Inebriated, wet and warm, life thrills in me
And slowly blazes to a bonfire of thrilling joys.

I am a poet,
Older than the crazy run of time,
And I fantasize in creating.

At a sweep of my thoughts, worlds and civilizations
rise and fall.
Stars stud the dark sky.
Planets bounce in empty space.

Suns rise and suns set.

Into my concoction, I throw in grains of wisdom and
colours
Smiles and tears, anger and peacefulness
Love and violence.

A bit of sunset and a bit of sunshine,
A splash of the babbling brook
Some scented flowers of the dew drenched valleys,
Add glows of tender star lights, and I stir.
Space, universes, worlds emerge, sprout and spread?

Know it whoever will
Love it whoever will.
I am the beginning and I am the end.
I am love, I am wisdom and I am ecstasy!
I am good and I am evil.

The glory of all glories, I am sunshine and I am
darkness.
Choose my sunny side
And inherit endless heritage of happiness.
From my dark side, tears follow.

Pull your curtains of Ignorance
And the stars of hope and light
The space, infinite and wondrous are a breath away.

Catch the marvel of my mystery, I dance

Fanning planets and starlight in the darksome space
An ecstatic dance of ceaseless creation!

Listen to my roar in the turbulent ocean
My laughter in the rowdy gales
The sounds of my transcendental flute.

Watch my glory in the sunset
And my joys in the sunrises.
In your own heart
Seek my peace in the untroubled ocean of serenity.

I never cease to give.
Seek me, the eternal giver and find in me eternal
repose
Those who are contented with taking what I give,
End in heartbreaks

For my gifts are ephemeral.
Seek me alone, child
And be for ever happy!

180

THE WAY TO PEACE

There is nothing
More beautiful than in the late afternoon,
Like sitting by oneself on the shore,
Eyes closed and heart open
To the thrills of the night come to roost.

I have seen them all before, I do not need to look
at them.
I could read them unfolding in my mind's eye.
I know around me, the colours are softly knitting
into each other
Creating a tissue of untrammeled fusion.

I know that the ripples,
Crowned with roving shimmers of blinking foams
Are drifting dazed towards the shore.
As the colours gently fizzle out,
A broad scatter of stars explode in the darkening
sky.

Sit quiet with me, I shall take you to the land of
peace
And light.
Let go of yourself and gently step into a place
You have never been before,
A land of infinity and enthralling beauty.

There is no pain there, no tears.
There, like flying tinsels, fireflies frolic in the
dark.
Remember those dreams that failed that you left
behind
Those tears that you shed?
They are there, whole waiting to be culled.

Build your picture of beauty inside.
Let the light
And the serenity that in frustration you lost
Come back

Open the door to new hope.
There the sun does not set
The ripples will cry
But there will be no tears.

The sea will rise and fall,
But there will be no violence
Build your hills and your mountains!

You may go one day and leave this place,
But you will never leave them behind again.
For there, there is no failure,
There is no success
Only you and you are eternal.

Your love is your contributions to this living
design.
One day long ago you came to build.
You lost your way, a slave to the senses
They will stay in your heart and point your soul
To the direction of eternity,
The immortal light!

They will lift you
And in moments of sadness, wipe your tears!
For He who made it all,
Left a little space for us to finish his design.
What you leave behind is what you will take with
you,
Good or bad!

I SHALL BE FOR EVER NEAR.

He said once
Wherever you are, call me.
Whatever you are doing, remember me!

Wherever you go, take me with you!
When it storms, I shall be your shelter.
In your loneliness I shall be your invisible friend,
Your comforter.

You may not see me,
But at night I shall be the stars
That light your path;
I shall be the gentle moonlight that smoothes your
restlessness,
The coolness that comforts your pain.

At daybreak I shall be your sunshine.
When your health fails,
The friend who whispers into your ears.
I am near, nearer to you
Than this world that is constantly slipping away.

I am waiting to give, friend.
My hands are full of gifts, are you strong enough
take them?
Seek from me the fulfilment of all your dreams.

Open then the gate to your heart,
And tell me, come in,
Come in.
Come and dine with you!

Through the doors of infinity
Have I called you.
I am the birds that wake you up
And the sea that lulls you!

I am the ancient hills and the mountains,
The woodlands and the flowers,
That breathe songs of eternal liberation
But you hear not!

Swayed by the tantalising senses,
Your eyes see me not,
Your heart waffles.
Your mind forgets me

I have been here, near you.
Now
Yesterday
And all the tomorrows, will be.

Even if you are let down by the world,
Friends deny you, I shall for ever be near,
By your side, I am the Ocean of mercy
Ever full of love
For ever again!

184

LOOK WHERE YOU ARE GOING

The knot of this creation is tied
With both good and bad, all made by him who made
them
The choice is ours and our choice is our way
To tears or to smiles.

There is good
And there is evil in this world,
A relative world, impermanent
Still I love this world, there is more to it
Than meet the eyes.

It is a place where gold, silver
And diamond lie silent in slime
And evil blazes forth loud trails of bloodshed.

Man could be a scorpion
Or a viper.
But from him, great saints and avatars are born.
I love him because there is in him the ultimate
truth
The place where in the middle of thorns, hate and
greed
Love, wisdom and beauty survive too,
Like breezes in the heart of gales...

The village pond could be treacherous,
The hill and mountains perilous,
Still I love them because of their serenity
In them are answers to questions man is bristling to
uncover.

There is nothing here that is not of His making,
All pieces to mount the cosmic mosaic.
They were never made to be traps,
More of blessings.

God gave us intelligence to discriminate
Sensitivity to love

And wisdom to choose rightly.

ANOTHER LEASE OF LIFE

A ray of sun light strays
Through the dark labyrinth of the village wood
And tickles a mighty breath of life,

Oh wonder of wonders!
Breeze begins to blow,
Leaves to strum
And birds rise from their nests singing pleasant
eulogies of praise.
Another lease of life is freely endowed.

I watch.
And I wonder from where life spring.
Such exuberance of ineffable beauty,
That blinds the senses.
What gives it that inexhaustible zest and vigour.

Wise men have wondered
But no answer found,
A great many books written,
Search in vain!

Great songs have been sung
With tearful hearts, full of devotion.
Heavens have been moved
Yet my friend, like rain, they all come down,
Ineffective!

He who knows the answer sits quiet,
Ages after ages,
In his abode of silence, waiting.
How dearly we want to reach up there!

And how dearly he wants us to reach up to him.
But guided by greed and false devotion,
Pride and ignorance
Our arrows always go the wrong way.

186

I WAITED

I waited all day and night for just one word of
love.
I waited for a week,
I waited for a month.
A whole year passed
But it never came.

The cold winter nights came
And dragged their feet in the wet windy darkness.
I waited.
My nose to the cold window pane,
Tearful and heavy hearted.

Night turned into day,
The mellow beams of the young sun
Kissed the bedewed garden slabs,
Shivered into thousand smithereens of sparkling
candle lights.
Waking the flowers from their slumbrous torpour.

I watched the tiny robin skip perkily, chasing
butterflies
And squirrels scuttling deftly on the wooden fence.
I waited.
Night again.

The same old silence, heavier, more unbearable,
A garland of led. I slept.

Shaken by the old wise man,
I woke up trembling like from a nightmare,
On fire, burning with despair and shame.

His last words before he left resounded
Like a whip on my conscience:
Child, life is like counting, you get from it what
you put into it.
Not a penny more, not a penny less.

I SALUTE YOU ARTIST

I salute you artist

Who can bring my master home to me.

Love they say has no language,
And no time to bloom
A single flower blooming in all the hearts
Always waiting,
Be it sun or storm.

I salute the heart that guides the hand
And the hand that guides the brush.
At the command of love,
The universe explodes in transcendental joy;

The heart thaws and the land is flooded
The mind, the brush and the oil
All merging into a perfect marriage.

No mortal can rise up to this miracle.
For perfection is only my master's own
exclusivity.
So I salute the hand
That could so faultlessly play the games of my
master.

With a few sweeps of your paint brush,
A universe is born.
Limitless space blooms
Earth, moon and sun adjust,
Million of stars twinkle in the dark sky,

All locked into an unimaginable and motionless
speed.
I salute you artist.
Given a little more inspiration,

The river would be running,
The trees swaying in the wind,
The sun rising
Behind those unruly skeins of clouds.

These birds are raring
To abandon themselves to the blue sky
From their colourful and exuberant oil perches.
I could feel
Their will to break free from this condemned
immobility.

My heart swells
I warm up.
Unshed tears prick my eyes.
I cry in joy at the marvel
My master has made of this place!

THE PLACE WHERE I WAS BORN

Across acres of land, mountains and oceans
Comes the voice of my mother,
The call of an endearing heart,
The place where I was born:

A flower of ineffable beauty,
Born from the torrid embrace of amorous billows
She dances in the laps of churning ripples;

Where the sun never sleeps,
Sunshine like woven garlands of gold
Lay gentle on slumbrous eyes,

Young sugar cane heave in gentle breeze
Hills and mountains vie to kiss the blue sky,
Where birds yodel, trill and choir, merry;
Where the air throbs with the sounds of tambourines.

Full bosomed,
Dressed in eternal green,
Lined with a frill of white sand
And turquoise sea, she blooms
in her sprawling shawl of embroidered flamboyant.

Whose face still haunts me,
After forty years of absence,
The same that cries now and in the past.
Little I knew, when as a child,
I romped down her rivers,
Climbed her trees,
Picking her wild fruits,

Enjoying her hills and mountains
And clinging to her frills of white sand
Little I knew that I would one day leave her
Shores and folds.

190

I remember my long walks
Lonely and scary through
Furling curtains of thick fog,
After the battering of a marauding storm,

And the pain still lingers.

Remembering the joys she freely gave me,
Here am I now in these lines
Offering my love and devotion at her feet
For no mother was ever born to be like her.

WHAT CAN I ASK YOU?

You often ask me if I wanted something.
I have never asked you for anything,
Because when I came home

After a long travel
Away from you and this place
And those I love,

My larder was already full
Brimming, no place for further replenishment.
This place was new, furbished and wondrous
The trees full of fruits,

The river running with pure water
The land fertile, always expecting
And the harvest was plenty.

Beautiful birds grace the blue sky
With their songs.

And I met my mother and father
And so many sweet smiling faces.

You made it all happen
Before I ever set foot here.
What more can I ask?

192

I WANT YOU TO FORGET

One day I shall not be here
To sing this song to you.
You will be alone.

The nights will be long and tearful
As the stars shed tears of tender light.
Your days lonely and endless
As long as the candle of memories
Burn in your heart
Remembering me;

This song I will leave for you.
This writing will remain
Braving time, life and painful memories.
This writing will bring me back;

And unseen, in the tender of the night
I will wipe your tears.
I will breathe comfort into your failing heart
And light the candles of happy smiles on your lips.

The night will be short again

You will not miss me then.
You will dare the tyranny of time.
This is my promise to you.

From the grave of sadness
The gentle sunshine will a new candle of hope
And inspire strength into your failing limbs
Your steps will be steadier.

Sometime even wisdom fail to light the path
Intended for two
Doubt and delusion then take over.

Bt you will forget.
You will forget,
I want you to forget.

SHARE MY LOVE

I give you love,
You may need it or you may not.

In dark, it will be your light.
In helplessness, your strength
And in pain, your comfort.

Forget the past.
Nebulous, buried into rusty pages of history,
Wrapped up in clammy dust, it sleeps

An irretrievable sleep.

Ahead is hope.
Hope is love.
Love is light and light, fearlessness.

This I give to you: a parcel of eternal
cheerfulness,
A universe spun in multifarious colours
Strewn with suns, moons and beaming stars,

Decked with valleys in bloom
Seething oceans and lively rivers,
Fertile lands,
A gift to cherish.

The mind will gnaw at it
And doubts will flaunt false and tempting baubles.
But this love will never fail, it will stand by you.

The stars will never stop to shine, the sun to rise
and to set,
Nor the hills and the mountains stop to bestow their
coolness.
For even the torrid desert sand, unsafe in its
magnanimity
Safeguards those who sadly stray in its rugged folds
And offer a bowl of clear water.

This is an elusive place, my friend,
As treacherous as the soft side of the hill,
Changing ceaselessly, hard to resist.
Only perfect love is eternal, immutable, the hunger
of the soul.

There is only love here.
Hate. hypocrisy and jealousy all go by the name of
love.
They are all shades of love.

But as darkness recedes at the rise of the sun
Hailing the advent of light
Thus birds of ill-omen flee at the approach of pure
love.

Until we find this ultimate and sublime love
My friend,
Share my love.